Three Princes Armed

Luxury Liners to Warships

To Alexander.

Enjoy ~ I have

R Q Darling far.

Robert Darlington
Fraser McKee

ISBN   978-0-9810274-0-1

Library and Archives Canada Cataloguing in Publication

Darlington, Robert A.
    Three princes armed : luxury liners to warships / Robert Darlington, Fraser McKee.

Includes bibliographical references and index.
ISBN 978-0-9810274-0-1

    1. Prince David (Ship)--History. 2. Prince Henry (Ship)--History.
3. Prince Robert (Ship)--History. 4. Canada. Royal Canadian
Navy--History--World War, 1939-1945. 5. Armed merchant
ships--Canada--History--20th century. 6. Landing craft--Canada--
History--20th century. 7. Warships--Canada--History--20th
century. 8. World War, 1939-1945--Naval operations, Canadian.
I. McKee, Fraser M., 1925- II. Title.
D779.C2D373 2008   940.54'5971   C2008-904077-5

Book design: bookdesign.ca
Printed in Canada

Contents

Previous Publications By The Authors

Fraser M. McKee

Volunteers For Sea Service, A Brief History of the RCNVR. Houston Standard Publications, Toronto 1973

The Armed Yachts of Canada, Boston Mills Press, Erin Ontario 1983

HMCS SWANSEA The Life and Times of a Frigate, Vanwell Publishing Ltd., St. Catherines, Ont., 1994

The Canadian Naval Chronicle 1939-1945, with R.A. Darlington, Vanwell Publishing Ltd., St. Catherines Ont., 1996 & 1998

Sink All The Shipping There, The Wartime Loss of Canada's Merchant Ships and Fishing Schooners. Vanwell Publishing Ltd., 2004

Robert A. Darlington

The Canadian Naval Chronicle 1939-1945, with Fraser M. McKee, Vanwell Publishing Ltd., St. Catherines Ont., 1996 & 1998

Front Cover: Photo of Prince David used as public relations for the movie Commandos Strike At Dawn. Copies were given to all members of the ship's company

Back Cover: Watercolour painting of Prince Robert by courtesy of wartime Able Seaman Bill Sloan, RCNVR of HMCS Morden now living in Stittsville, Ontario. The painting was commissioned by Gary McGregor of Delta, B.C. whose father Martin served in the Robert as a Telegraphist and was on board when his ship was at the liberation of Hong Kong in 1945.

Preface and Acknowledgements

APART FROM THE NAVAL CONNECTION of the two authors, the genesis of this tale arose out of a published request by the naval magazine "Warship International" in 1968 for someone to prepare for one of their issues an article on the Royal Canadian Navy's wartime *Prince* Class ships. They had served as Armed Merchant Cruisers, Landing ships and an AA cruiser. Fraser McKee had been editing a couple of naval officers' newsletters and had enjoyed the contacts that arose, so volunteered.

At that time many of the participants, particularly the more senior ones – Captains, Commanders, senior Chief Petty Officers, even most of the commanding Admirals - were still around to be contacted. The important thing, he soon appreciated, was to go beyond the elementary ships' log books and Commanding Officers' monthly 'Reports of Proceedings'. It was clear enough what the ships had done, where they had gone, what had been accomplished. But those are weak reeds upon which to lean – they tell what the writers wanted their superiors to know – Commanding Officers for the logs, Admirals and Captains (D) for the Reports of Proceedings. What was required to make the article a living tale, more than just a recitation of the ships' movements, were the personal inputs. It was all very well to talk to seamen, stokers, sub-lieutenants – the younger set - but, from his own experience in ocean escorts, Fraser soon found they rarely knew the "why" of events. "I know where you went, and what you did. What I need to know is why that decision was made? How did you feel as that happened? What was Commander Bloggins <u>really</u> like? I don't want to say that he was beloved by all his crew when he was, in fact, a most objectionable s.o.b.! In the final history I need not say so, but should avoid the worst errors of description."

So, fortunately, the basics of the story were researched and collected – the log book entries, plus many interviews, letters, small reports, the personal recollections. An article resulted in 1970, on "Princes Three." There were, therefore, files in Fraser's attics (he moved a couple of times), two large box files. But there they sat, while he went on to write or co-write four books on other naval subjects.

~ ~ ~

There is always a reason for a book. In our case it was quite simple. We enjoyed the opportunity to work on the project, the second time we have done this, and since the navy has always been part of our lives, we would like others to share in that. When we collaborated on "The Canadian Naval Chronicle – 1939-1945" it was not alone for the veterans who had been in the Navy those years. We had in mind the children and grandchildren of those vets who maybe knew Dad or Grandfather had been in an action at sea but rarely talked about it. Time and again a son or daughter would say to us, after Dad had passed away, "He never wanted to talk about his time in the Navy. His stories died with him untold." As well we thought the general reader should be aware of the Navy's **successes** as well as the losses commemorated on Remembrance Day – all too often the only "remembrances." For the younger generation the war was often just something in history books. Hopefully "Chronicle" filled in some of the background.

For the three *Prince* ships the rationale is somewhat different. They were not sunk, were rarely in any engagements where they were in serious danger, and only one captured an enemy vessel. Because of this they are always given little attention in the bibliography of the RCN. They were "different", outside the mainstream of Jim Lamb's "Corvette Navy" or of the dashing destroyers in the English Channel battles. And because they were different their story needs to be inserted as part of the broad seascape of the Canadian Navy at war. Except for the Indian Ocean and most of the South Atlantic they left their wakes in most of this earth's waters. They often sailed alone. But when they were in company it was for great events. Like the D-Day landings in Normandy, in the Aleutians being retaken by the Americans, and in the surrender of the Japanese at Hong Kong.

They were generally successful in their missions, although in retrospect fortunate in never meeting a potentially lethal foe. At the time they were "home" to many sailors – probably over 5,000 in all. Many of those men were pleased to be interviewed, relive their youth as seamen, share their memories, loan papers, letters and photographs. Sadly, many who did so over the past 30 years have not lived to see the book about events of over 60 years ago. By mentioning many of the participants we wanted the book to have the personal touch – the Navy is more than steel ships, log book entries and calendar facts. The book does not contain much new and original research. It is a synthesis of the three ships' adventures, lives lived, the Navy "passing on the seas on its lawful occasions," as the Naval prayer puts it. For the same reason reference notes are kept to a minimum, as they are disruptive when a story is being told. This is not an academic exercise. It is Canadian history.

In the early 1990s Fraser worked on a book, "The Canadian Naval Chronicle" with the co-author of this one, Bob Darlington. Then recently, knowing Fraser had been interested in those *Princes*, Bob suggested they were well worth a more complete treatment due to their interesting pre-war lives and wartime varied careers. With much good-natured prodding and negotiating as to who would do what portion, Bob finally got the effort on the rails and under way. He agreed to do most of the wartime part, based on both Fraser's files of 35 years before and much new material from DND's Directorate of History and Heritage (DHH). Fraser would do the pre-war and post-war parts of the history. Thus this story came to pass.

As neither of us served in these ships (although Fraser as a young teenager was aboard *Prince Henry*, then the *North Star* at Pictou, Nova Scotia), all depended on a wide range of sources. Official published sources of Canadian naval history were the vital frame on which all depended, such as Joseph Schull's "The Far Distant Ships" and the brand new two volume series sponsored by DHH - "No Higher Purpose" and "A Blue Water Navy." Many other histories and biographies have added detail and colour to the story. These include histories of Sir Henry Thornton and of the Canadian National Railways; on British troop transports; on the Normandy invasion and that at the South of France and in the Aleutians. There were also valuable references found in Navy Lists, David Freeman's "Canadian Warship Names" and a host of others, noted in the credits.

But the life of the story, for this is not just about steel ships and engines, but about crews, real living people, some of whom died in these events, came from letters, interviews, reports, e-mails and recollections of those who did serve in the three ships. Their names as well are in the Credits. While the telling of the story is the responsibility of the authors, many of the stories quoted are as remembered, sometimes after as much as 70 years by participants, so there may be unintentional errors or misplacements. That remains the authors' responsibility for not being able to ensure complete accuracy. But they set the tone, make the ships come alive, and for that we are highly grateful. The story could not have been told without them.

Another basic dependency for this history, in particular the wartime years, is contained in a DHH 365-page history written in 1965 by Malcolm Macleod just for their files. This major work was noted by CDR Colin Darlington, who also helped on several other occasions to move the tale along and to provide useful editing. Macleod's history could have stood alone as the *Princes'* story, except it was somewhat too long, had 30-odd appendices in extensive detail "for the record." But we fully appreciate the easy, often entertaining tone of his narrative, and have made much use of it to ensure what appears here conforms with what DND knew of their history more than 45 years ago.

The CNR history came from many internet CNR sites, from D'Arcy Marsh's somewhat roseate biography of Sir Henry Thornton, and assistance from the CN's then-historians, Colonel G.R. Stevens and Dr. Ken Mackenzie. It is a most complicated history of financial successes and failures, political intrigues and pressures, a story of Canada's fantastic early growth as a unified nation, and of bitter rivalries. Only the briefest of coverage appears here. The post-war *Princes'* histories depend largely on journals of maritime organizations interested in passenger ships and troop transports. Interpretations of those histories are of course Fraser McKee's.

In the preparation of the text we are most appreciative of the careful reviews thereof by Commander (S) Al Tassie and Richard Bentham, an ex-RCAF and civilian test pilot. Without their correcting notes many errors would have remained, the text potentially full of abstruse "navalese." The watercolour painting of *Prince Robert* which graces the back cover was painted by Bill Sloan, a wartime Coder who served on board HMCS *Morden*. We are grateful for his permission to use it.

And yet again the two authors are highly appreciative of the help and forbearance of their wives during the gestation. They both contributed ideas and cautions, and put up with long absences at our computer terminals. Nothing of ours would get written without them.

Robert Darlington, Victoria
Fraser McKee, Toronto
May, 2008

Prologue and Raison D'etre

*"Oh Lord, Thou knowest how busy we must be this day; if we forget
Thee, do not Thou forget us. For Christ's sake, Amen"*
Colonel of Horse, Sir Jacob Astley's prayer
before the Battle of Edgehill, 1642.

The large camouflaged gray painted passenger liner moved slowly forward in a brisk warm breeze and modest green-gray seas on a hazy early morning. The land, somewhat more than seven miles ahead and rather flat, with few easily identified landmarks or buildings, was largely covered in a roiling cloud of dust, smoke and explosions, from slightly to the ship's left to its the far right. Between the ship and the shore a destroyer steamed slowly across from left to right, firing furiously with all her heavier guns at some inland target. Other small landing craft were moving inward or outward from the beaches.

Although aboard the ship it was unnaturally quiet with only the odd shouted order or seaman-like bos'n's pipe, the air was thrumming with the sound of aircraft overhead, the thump of distant heavy gunfire and the remote concussions of battle. The ship, while extensively modified from its peacetime configuration still looked handsome and efficient, with four large Assault Landing Craft (LCA) suspended on either side from massive davits occupying about half the ship's length. They gave the ship an appearance of a large beetle with its wing covers only partly opened.

On the open bridge, the Navigator, standing close behind the central compass binnacle, alternated between trying to identify shore buildings across the pelorus and listening to a nearby voicepipe from the radar office behind and below him.

"Eleven thousand four hundred, Sir." "Very good."

He repeated this range offshore to the Captain, standing quietly at the front of the bridge ten feet ahead of him, looking steadily through large binoculars at the shore over the windscreen. All on the bridge, eleven or twelve seamen, petty officers and officers, were wearing dark blue life vests over their uniforms and dark blue steel helmets. The Captain was identified by white lettered "CAPT" across the back of his helmet. This warlike preparedness was the requirement in Daily Orders, although they were a bit self-conscious at such unusual military preparedness. The only exception was two khaki battledress clad infantry Army officers, their regiments identified by subdued patches on their shoulders, Queen's Own Rifles and Régiment de la Chaudière. They stood a bit to one side, also peering at the distant land through small infantry binoculars. They wore khaki steel helmets, no life jackets but several items like gas mask haversacks, map cases, pistols and other odd pieces clipped onto their field service webbing.

Without turning, the Captain called out "Dead slow ahead." The Officer of the Watch, a Lieutenant, leaned over another voicepipe to the wheelhouse – "Dead slow ahead", listened for a response. "Dead slow ahead, Sir."

From radar: "Ten thousand eight hundred yards, Sir." "Very good."

The Captain again – "Stop engines." Repeated to the wheelhouse. A watchful pause, all eyeing the turmoil ahead. Not exactly apprehensive, but cautious, prepared... for something. None of them yet knew for sure what the morning would bring. They tended to avoid each other's eye, although each glanced at the Captain from time to time, resolute, calm, not given to outward emotion.

"Slow astern", again quietly repeated. The Captain stepped onto a small platform in the starboard forward corner of the bridge, took a small green flag on a two foot stick out of a bracket on the side of the bridge and held it high over his head, looking now down onto the foc's'le 100 feet in front of him.

There the First Lieutenant stood in the eyes of the ship, facing the bridge, with an Able Seaman holding a sledge hammer handle, its heavy iron head resting on the deck. He stood braced against the gentle rolling just to one side of the starboard anchor cable, watching alternately the officer and the distant scene ahead. On the anchor winch, set a few yards further aft, a Stoker Petty Officer also faced forward, his hand on a lever with a small handle on the top extending up from the starboard drum of the winch around which the massive cable passed. He, in the manner of most engine-room types reacting to upper deck regulations, had elected to wear as usual a rather scruffy P.O.'s cap, not his "tin hat", for which the First Lieutenant had castigated him. The explanation "Forgot about it, Sir" was, under the circumstances, allowed, with "Well you shouldn't have" just to establish the necessary authority.

On the distant bridge the Captain's anchoring flag suddenly dropped and the First Lieutenant shouted "Slip!" The seaman hoisted his sledge, clouted the Blake slip link holding the anchor cable taught; the tooth cracked back and with a clanging roar of iron shackles the cable ran across the metal plate on the deck and down the hawsehole, the anchor splashing into the sea. The First Lieutenant leaned over the foc's'le rail, watching the cable run out for a few seconds, then, as the ship began to move slowly astern and the anchor settled onto the gravelly bottom, indicated to the bridge with his arm the angle forward and outward of the cable.

On the bridge the Captain ordered "Stop engines", returned his small flag to its holder, waited until the ship seemed to be riding comfortably to its cable, stepped down off his vantage point, turned and said quietly to the Navigator "See if you can get a good fix and be sure to mark it on the chart." To the Officer of the Watch: "Tell the Engineroom we'll keep at 'stand by' for now until we see what's going on." He paused, looked again at the scene ahead, then turned to the two Army officers.

"Well, there you are. Sorry it isn't a bit closer in. Now it's your turn. The best of good fortune to you. To all of you."

"Thank you Captain," one replied, both saluting. "You've been very good to us. We'll see you again, I hope." They quickly turned, went down off the bridge and aft.

The Captain walked to the after starboard corner of the bridge. There he looked aft to where the Executive Officer, a Commander also in life jacket and helmet, was standing just forward of the foremost nested landing craft, looking expectantly up at the bridge.

"Lower away" called down the Captain, acknowledged by the X.O. with a wave of his arm - "Lower away." The X.O. turned to loudly repeat the order to the seamen manning the eight massive davits and falls on each side of the vessel, his order being passed aft by others waiting. At each craft, as the davit slowly rocked outward and each Landing Craft Assault dropped down a few feet to just below deck level. Soldiers in their khaki uniforms, burdened with rifles, 60-pound packs, mortar bits and pieces, Bren machine guns and other unidentified Army paraphernalia, began to clamber over the side and into the swaying craft. The two officers from the bridge shook hands a bit self-consciously and joined their appointed LCAs on either side of the ship. All had been offered an excellent breakfast, an indication of the ship's distant past as a first class passenger ferry, although few had felt much like participating, given the less than smooth crossing during the night and their high apprehension about the day's future events.

It was just after 8 a.m., the early morning of June 6th, 1944. HMCS *Prince David* and her sister ship *Prince Henry*, also anchored about a mile away, now called Landing Ships Infantry (Medium), had arrived off the shore of Normandy. They were part of Operation Neptune, in these waters the Royal Navy's most massive and vital naval event since Trafalgar 139 years before. Landing their 500 troops was to fully justify their existence, although it had often not been foretold.

~ ~ ~

Fourteen months later, half a world away from the turmoil of Normandy, another very similar ship, in fact a sister ship of the two anchored off the French coast, very similarly slid quietly through the debris cluttered waters of Hong Kong harbour. She moved toward a series of wharves jutting out from a projecting headland of the Kowloon shore on the mainland, opposite the island itself. Apart from some very distant shouting it was, compared to Normandy, eerily quiet and still.

But this ship had no landing craft, being more prosaically armed with five sets of twin four-inch HA/LA gun mountings, 40 mm pom-poms and several Oerlikons at various locations across her decks and bridge. All were fully manned and loaded, and the guns were being trained slightly from side to side, just to ensure all was operating – in case of need. Here too there was some apprehension, for as at Normandy no one was sure exactly what would transpire. Instead of pointing upwards to fend off aircraft, as was their original role, all the guns were leveled at the land ahead. Technically the Pacific war was ended, but one never knew if the message had reached distant outposts.

The Captain and crew, appropriately dressed in spotless white summer uniforms, shorts and white stockings, open-necked shirts, this time without steel helmets or life vests, watched the wharves and shore ahead through binoculars. There, a confused mass of humanity behind wire barricades at the shore end of the wharves were shouting at green-clad and armed Japanese soldiers working at loading various material onto a scruffy small freighter lying farther up on the opposite side of Holt's Wharf. The city behind gave off a miasma of smoke, smell and dust. There was a sense of muted turmoil, with crowds milling about in all the streets leading to and along the sea front and on some of the other wharves.

On the ship's bridge, the Captain looked aft over his left shoulder, out into the main stream, where a purposeful large cruiser and several destroyers were also slowing to anchor there, wanting to be sure his ship would be within signaling visibility and gunnery protection of them.

"Starboard side to. Dead slow ahead. Port twenty" he told the Officer of the Watch who repeated the order to the wheelhouse and others below, causing a bustle along the ship's upper deck forward and aft as fenders were slung over and mooring lines looped over the rails. The ship slid slowly in a curve toward the left side of the outer end of the wharf.

Turning to a Lieutenant with webbing equipment over his whites standing nearby behind him, also watching events ashore, the Captain commented quietly: "Whittal, as soon as lines are ashore get your parties onto the jetty, ready for anything. Stop those geezers doing whatever it is they're at, and secure the shore end of the jetty. Tell me what's up via your runner, and we'll sort out the next step." "Aye aye, Sir," and the officer hurried off the bridge.

The ship eased slowly alongside the wharf with a slight bump, seamen jumped ashore from the lower after section of the ship, their attention divided between handling the lines, throwing the heavy loops over bollards on the jetty and keeping a weather eye on the two mobs 150 yards up the jetty. They seemed to pay them no mind. Soon a group of almost 100 fully armed and webbed Seamen under a few officers, a Warrant Gunner, Chiefs and Petty Officers, all commanded by the Lieutenant flowed over the ship's side at various points onto the planking of the jetty. There they formed into loose but orderly squads, unslinging their rifles, fixing the bayonets for effect and checking the rifle magazines to ensure they were loaded.

On the bridge the Captain, in exactly the same form as had happened off Normandy, said to the Officer of the Watch, "Tell the Engineroom we'll keep at stand by for now until we see what's going on." They all remained on the bridge, alternately looking at events ashore and ensuring they were covered by the other ships anchoring in the harbour. No soldiers on the bridge on this occasion. The squads on the jetty gripped their rifles and moved purposefully shoreward.

Thus HMCS *Prince Robert* arrived at Hong Kong, not for the first time, and this time to atone for a most unfortunate duty the same ship had performed there three and a half years before. This time, in a couple of days, they were to lift the souls and spirits of a group of emaciated surviving Canadian soldiers who had not seen a friendly Canadian face in those three years.

Foreword

Bob Darlington and Fraser McKee have brought the fascinating story of three little known Canadian ships out of the shadows. To say that Canada was ill prepared when war came in 1939 is an understatement. Expansion of the tiny (its personnel including Reserves numbered under 3,000) Royal Canadian Navy was urgent. The three Canadian National Steamships *Princes* were improvised warships which typify how Canada hurriedly constructed a navy to meet operational demands. They were small passenger liners converted to become "Armed Merchant Cruisers" and initially armed with obsolescent guns, a response to a threat from enemy merchant raiders perceived before the war. The imaginative conversion plans by civilian naval architects gave the *Princes* an appearance remarkably similar to that of a purpose built warship. In fact, like other Armed Merchant Cruisers the trio were vulnerable to attack and had other defects as fighting ships. They nevertheless would prove their usefulness in a variety of roles as the long Second World War ground on. All three were modified during the conflict for new tasks – two to carry landing craft and one as an anti-aircraft cruiser.

While the main contribution of the Royal Canadian Navy to victory was in anti-submarine warfare Canada also contributed forces to many other missions. The three *Princes* were the largest Canadian warships until the RCN acquired a light cruiser and manned an auxiliary aircraft carrier in 1944. When the first conversion, *Prince Robert*, commissioned as a warship in mid 1940 the composition of her crew reflected the manpower then available. More than half of her officers were ex merchant service as were thirty percent of her ratings. Just under twenty percent were experienced permanent force men but almost half of the "lower deck" had just completed their initial training. As the RCN began growing rapidly the percentages of those who had joined for hostilities only soon came to predominate. The authors estimate that 5,000 men served in these three ships. For many they provided the first formative experiences of naval service at sea.

The *Princes* roamed from the Aleutians, to the Mediterranean and Aegean. They escorted convoys against surface and air threats across the Pacific and in the eastern Atlantic. Their contributions to operations far from Canada outline how the Allies were able to use sea power to project their land forces. They landed Allied troops including Canadians on D-Day, in southern France and Greece. *Prince Robert* not only transported Canadian troops to Hong Kong in late 1941 but also was part of the task force that liberated the colony in 1945 and helped to succour the emaciated soldiers who had survived as POWs.

The story of these three ships before, during and after the war is one of adaptation to changing wartime operational circumstances as well as adaptation to changing economic factors in the use of commercial shipping. It illustrates the "can do" ethos of the Canadian Navy. Captain Darlington and Commander McKee have drawn on the reminiscences of wartime sailors to illustrate how varied were the tasks accomplished by these three improvised warships. Their coverage of amphibious landings also casts light on how the Canadian manned landing craft operated. All of this is a welcome look at how Canadians rose to unanticipated challenges.

Jan Drent, Commodore Ret'd.
Victoria, BC, March 2008

(Commodore Drent joined the RCN in 1954. He served in a number of ships and commanded HMC Ships *Annapolis*, *Qu'Appelle* and *Provider*. His shore appointments included CF Staff College, RN Staff College, Canadian Naval Attache Moscow, Helsinki and Warsaw, Deputy Saclant and Cincan Representative at NATO HQ Brussels. He retired to Victoria in 1990 where he pursues and writes naval history)

CHAPTER ONE

Thornton
The Empire Builder

*Is it so bad, then, to be misunderstood? Pythagoras was misunder-
stood, and ... Newton and every wise spirit that ever took flesh. To
be great is to be misunderstood."*
                    Ralph Waldo Emerson "Essays" (1841)
                                        'Self Reliance'

THE THREE *PRINCE* SHIPS OF THIS TALE, rather too early in their eventual careers, were described in D'Arcy Marsh's sympathetic 1935 biography as "Sir Henry Thornton's last extravagance." They certainly contributed to his eventual downfall and dismissal from the Canadian National Railway's system. The three players in this history, the man, the railway and the ships were interdependent, so one cannot understand the "why" of the ships without a brief look at the other two.

If ever there was a Canadian nation builder who is almost completely unknown, it must be Sir Henry Worth Thornton, KBE. He was not really a "Canadian" for he was born in Logansport, Indiana, made his initial reputation with American railways, gained his KBE in Britain through his efforts there and in France during the first World War, died in New York City and is buried in Newtown, Pennsylvania. But his bust still appears on plaques in several Canadian railway stations and in hotels such as in

Halifax, and there is a Thornton rail yard near Vancouver, testifying to his enthusiastic espousal and contributions to the country's development.

For almost 11 years, flamboyant and charismatic, even autocratic, Sir Henry dominated Canadian railway affairs. He introduced the first North American diesel locomotives, built hotels that are models to this day, established the first Canadian national broadcast radio, expanded the CNR's world shipping business, and fought with both its bitter rival Canadian Pacific Railroad and his masters, the Canadian Government. He was, as the saying goes, bigger than life and ahead of his time. And the *Prince* ships were both a high point and part of the tragedy that was to eventually engulf Sir Henry.

Born in November 1871 to a successful family, he was educated at Concord, New Hampshire, and at the University of Pennsylvania where "Hank" Thornton played senior rugby football, was selected All American, and even briefly coached the Vanderbilt University team in Tennessee. On graduation as a civil engineer at the University of Pennsylvania in 1894, he joined the Pennsylvania Railroad, initially as a draftsman. He rose rapidly through the ranks, as an Assistant engineer of construction at the Cleveland and Marietta Railway, a subsidiary of the "Pennsy", and in 1911 was moved to another subsidiary, the Long Island Rail Road, where he became the road's operating General Superintendent. Based on his work there he gained an increasing reputation throughout the industry for unconventionality in solving railroading operational problems. By this time he was married, to Virginia Blain, whom he was to divorce after his move to Canada in the 1920s.

In 1914 the Great Eastern Railroad (the GER) in Britain was having operating difficulties and looking for someone to take over and sort out their problems. They operated a major commuter rail system into London and had interlocking passenger ferry schedules moving their customers across to Europe. At the urging of

Lord Claud Hamilton, an MP for Kensington South London and Chairman of the Great Eastern and other railroads, Thornton's name came up as a competent, dynamic railway system manager. The Board of that company had the rather remarkable foresight to look beyond not only their own industry but the United Kingdom for a potential solution.

Henry Thornton, at only 43 years, was offered the job as General Manager of GER, and being open to a larger and different challenge, he accepted with little hesitation and moved to London with his family. The position included not only the commuter rail system serving the very busy complex northeast of the London area but incorporated that railroad's steamships from Harwich and other ports to the Continent. This was to have an echo almost 37 years later with one of his *Prince* ships after the Second World War that was to serve on that route. His approaches were, for the day, novel, as he even provided chairs for union representatives when they met in negotiations with the GER's Board of directors. This was maybe offset by another news reference to Thornton as "an unpopular alien!" But not with the railroadmen.

He had no more than taken over and instituted his improvements when the war started. Thornton was drawn into the British Army and appointed a Colonel as Assistant Director of Movements and Railways. He proved his worth in organizing the movement of tens of thousands of troops of the British Expeditionary Force around the United Kingdom, synchronizing their advance across the Channel and in France and Belgium. He was appointed Inspector General of Transportation and promoted to Major General. Thornton finished the war as such, spending much of his time and energy actually in the field and on the ships, ensuring the system operated with maximum efficiency, even if the terminals led to the horrific killing fields of France. He was awarded a knighthood in the Order of the British Empire for his services to the crown, and in France met the lady who was to become his second wife. He was by 1919 a naturalized British subject, possibly assuming he would be remaining in Britain.

By 1922, back with Great Eastern, that firm was being merged with several other British railways, and the now Sir Henry was on the lookout for another challenge, having reservations about the proposed amalgamation's future prospects. This time the move was to be back across the Atlantic to Canada. If he had been able to see more clearly the political maneuvering into which he was stepping, he might have been wise to search elsewhere. But in a speech to Toronto's Empire Club right after arrival in December, 1922 he included the comment "There are those of us who aspire higher, and endeavor to conquer the snow-clad heights of Mount Everest." A most prophetic comment - metaphorically he almost did.

~ ~ ~

Canada then was ideal for rail service, with huge distances, sparse populations and since the mid-1800s a new and rapidly growing country. Western settlement was government policy. The Canadian National Railways' primary predecessor, the Grand Trunk Railroad, was incorporated in 1852, starting between Montreal and Toronto but spreading east and west. With the Government giving land grants and loan guarantees the line was still then a private general stock company. In 1858, nine years before Canadian Confederation, British Columbia became a Crown Colony, and those representing the British government felt a transcontinental railway would bind the new colonies together – and prevent American squatters from seizing territory before Canadians had a chance. After Confederation the same attitude applied to bringing and keeping P.E.I and the other Maritime Provinces into the new Dominion. Railroads would be the linking chain to bring and hold the outposts of the Dominion.

But already the GTR gave its investors the impression of being a losing venture, shortly unable to pay dividends and threatening to default on its bonds. Not to follow this national road's highly complicated fortunes too closely, it acquired a series of presidents, appointed by various Boards and Governments' interventions. The first president, John Ross, was also a senior government official. A change to "Canadian" government in 1867 further complicated the issue, with varying aims as to the future for intercontinental rail expansion, and without the sufficient internal finances to accomplish this. In fact, in the later years of the century the Grand Trunk largely concentrated on expansion in Eastern Canada, often by acquisition of small local branch lines. The government of Sir John A. Macdonald even gave up on its support for the GTR and contracted with the privately owned and largely British funded Canadian Pacific Railroad to build the first connection through to the West coast. GTR stockholders hired a succession of American and English Presidents to try to get their company back on track financially. It is a bit difficult to appreciate how vital these trans-Canada lines were. For instance, to the silk trade from the Orient: raw silk was perishable, dedicated "Silk Trains" took precedence and traveled at up to 90 miles an hour. Insurance increased by 6% per hour if these trains were delayed reaching destinations in Ontario and Montreal.

The first decade or so of the 20th century marked a tremendous expansion of rail service right across Canada, and enthusiasm for railroads reached remarkable heights, with greater mileage per capita than in any country on earth. Expansion seemed to be an end in itself. The railroads owned exclusive tracts of land larger than many European countries. To justify their reach, expenses and continuing expansion, the larger ones advertised in those countries for settlers – to be carried and supplied by railroads, of course. The CPR established major steamship services to the Far East, the *Empress* liners, to bring passengers to the West Coast, thence by their railroad, completed in 1895, across Canada, and, if they so wished, by further CP ships across the Atlantic to Europe – the

"All Red Route." With the continuing growth opportunities and excellent advertising promotion, it was comparatively easy for the CP, and others, to borrow money in London to finance this expansion.

In comparison to the hard-nosed stock and bond-holder driven CPR operation, the Canadian National Railway, not in existence under that name until 1920, was a mare's nest of huge financial trouble and intricacy. This earlier story of the three *Prince* ships of the CNR depends to quite an extent on those difficulties, and while it has taken several books to cover the CN's history and background, a little more is needed here to set the scene. The CNR was formed just after the 1st War through firstly the integration and nationalization of two large mostly eastern-based railroads, the Canadian Northern and the Grand Trunk, who had on their books some $1.3 billion in loans – in 1922 dollars! In the 1880s the GTR had concentrated more on north-south traffic, in meat and grain, with the US, which was not in accord with the Canadian government's wishes.

To some extent for political expediency, the Government was forced into supporting several railways serving the west before the turn of the century, very much in competition with the CPR. The larger road was the Government's Grand Trunk Pacific Railway which spanned the West from Winnipeg to Prince Rupert by 1914, and on that coast owned a series of smaller ships serving the outports. But with few local branch lines, unlike the CP, it could not manage to cover its debt expenses. It was no coincidence of financial problems that the Panama Canal was opened in the same year, providing further competition to transcontinental rail travel. It was no longer "The only way to cross." The same applied to a more northerly transcontinental route, the Canadian Northern Railway, opened to the west coast in 1915. Both had to rely on Dominion Government loans, although they were still technically private railroads. In addition to those two, there were also the

Intercolonial Railway, the National Transcontinental Railway, and the more easterly Grand Trunk Railway itself, all having financial difficulties. In 1916, in all too typical Canadian fashion to this day, a Royal Commission was appointed to enquire into various options available. The Commission was under A.H. Smith, the president of the New York Central Railroad, a Canadian Commissioner Sir Henry Drayton, and an English railway authority, A.C. Acworth. Railway stock was considered a bell-wether of a country's financial health, so the Commission's responsibility was far more than finding a way to keep railways operating. It's decisions could easily affect Canada's whole credit rating abroad, especially in England.

A majority report of the Commission (Smith did not wholly agree) recommended that the Government take over the Grand Trunk, the Grand Trunk Pacific and many of the others and operate them as one system. While there were vehement arguments against the Government running a railway, particularly of course from the CPR, this seemed the only way to continue the lines, which was politically an imperative. With few major highways in good condition, the areas served could hardly just be abandoned. It could thus even allow for maintenance and prevent bankruptcy, ensure Canadian credit was protected, back the monies already loaned to the railroads, and, some said, prevent a CP monopoly across the country. In 1917 an Act was passed to acquire the Canadian Northern and the Grand Trunk. The CNR was formally established as of 6 June 1919.

Grand Trunk Pacific got into further financial problems that threatened receivership by 1919 so they too were nationalized by being transferred to the Board of Directors of the now Government controlled Canadian National Railways in February 1920. This included not only the railways themselves, but some hotels, ships and a telegraph system. The ships, formed into the Canadian Government Merchant Marine also in 1919, were vessels built on the Government's behalf during the boom shipping years of the

War, now managed as CNR's shipping division, Canadian National Steamship Services (CNSS). The amalgamation brought together over 90 different railways, to be divided into four operating regions – Atlantic, Central, Western (headquartered in Winnipeg) and Grand Trunk Western with headquarters in Detroit, Michigan. David B. Hanna was the first director, and at once began a reha-bilitation of not only the roadbeds and rolling stock but to look for new markets and actively compete with the CPR. One of his aims was to "Keep it out of politics." But Hanna was considered a bit too low key, a lawyer administrator, to be a dynamic new President. It was into this new and quite shaky venture that Henry Thornton stepped in 1922.

Sir Henry Thornton (right) of the CNR and Edward Beatty of the CPR in Toronto 15 November 1923.
Courtesy Toronto Globe and Mail

With the Canadian

Government searching for a president to take over the newly formed CNR and all its subsidiaries, their search became known world-wide, with suggestions from various sources. Even David Beatty, the lawyer-turned-President of the CPR, tentatively suggested Thornton, and Jimmy Thomas of the British Union of Railwaymen with whom he had been dealing in labour negotiations suggested directly to him he might like the job and told him something of the CNR's scope. So in October 1922, Sir Henry took himself by ship across to New York and up to Ottawa and was seen by Mackenzie King, the Prime Minister. The PM not only explained the job with some enthusiasm but assured Thornton that he would be able to operate the railroad as he saw fit, and "that so far as his Government was concerned no political influence would be brought to bear." While not necessarily an outright lie, King naturally avoided explaining how this would, or even could, be achieved. This was a major and certainly inaccurate assurance that was to dog the CNR. Now either Sir Henry was naïve, believing a country much younger than that from which he had just come and with a new and major rail system of its own could hardly be a problem, or presumed in his self confidence and air of authority he could dominate any petty politics. Or maybe he just trusted King's calm assurances – a major error in judgment of that wily fox.

At any rate, Sir Henry accepted the job. There seem to have been no other major contenders, and in December he and his family sailed across again and entrained for Ottawa. At 51, as his biographer D'Arcy Marsh put it, "Thornton was full of tremendous vigour, and had a restless urge to develop and expand the CNR." It had 22,000 miles of track and 100,000 employees, all from various previous roads, so far with no sense of common purpose. Thornton set out to change that. The CPR Board, and especially David Beatty, their president, felt that as the country's largest single taxpayer, it was unfair for the Government to be supporting only their competition. They had rather hoped to take over the foundering railroads, but the 1917 Report had killed that possibility. But it set that company firmly as a direct competitor with the CNR.

Thornton seized on his appointment as president of to be national railway to give speeches throughout the country and was soon, in many eyes, certainly his own, an unofficial ambassador for general growth, development and expansion across the Dominion beyond just that of "his" railway. He continued his efforts begun in Long Island and England of working harmoniously with all the employees from trackmen to vice-presidents to instill a feeling of pride and accomplishment for the CNR's purposes. He made trips to the US, to Britain and Europe to promote not only the railway but the country as a whole. He tried to avoid directly antagonizing his chief rival, the CP – what was past was past. Both were highly dependant on freight rates, unlike the Great Eastern Railroad which had primarily been involved with the mass movement of passengers in and out of London. But freight rates were in turn almost entirely a politically sensitive affair, and dared not be increased to solve the CN's inherited capital financial woes. While Thornton was part of the railway, **was** the railway from the roadbeds and workmen up, Beatty was a lawyer, a financier and really represented his financial backers, those who owned that railway. The two were quite different in temperament and outlook, although their aims for their roads were quite similar. The CP made money, the CN did not, in the overall.

Despite this instability of his base, Thornton worked enthusiastically for expansion and competition, many projects giving rise to later criticism. By 1929 he had expanded the CN up to the Hudson's Bay port of Churchill with a view of handling the minerals from Flin Flon mines and grain from Saskatchewan and the west. After all, it was the shortest route to Europe – when not iced in. He arranged to have built large hotels, in cities like Ottawa, Saskatoon, Victoria. Even built one in Halifax, which already had a CP-supported hotel, The Lord Nelson. There, despite negotiations started with CP for joint operation and ownership, he backed off, erecting an even larger one on the waterfront, The Nova Scotian, to directly serve shipping, particularly the CNSS's *Lady* boats. The hotels supported the railway, and *vice versa*.

By the time Thornton took over, shipping was an integral part of the CNR. With the rail system he had inherited the Canadian Government's Merchant Marine passenger and freight services. This included the quite successful Canadian National Steamship's subsidized service to the West Indies, served in the mid-1920s by now inefficient war built ships. In 1927, determined to improve the service, add passengers, and with new agreements between Canada and the West Indies governments, Thornton contracted for six larger and handsome new ships of two slightly different sizes to serve those routes, the imposing white *Lady* boats. The second Lady Thornton, Martha Watriss, even was the christening sponsor of one of the first, the *Lady Drake*, built by Cammell Laird & Co. in Birkenhead, across the Mersey from Liverpool, as were the later *Princes*.

This eye to expansion and competition led naturally to Thornton looking at the CP's successful monopoly on the West Coast, with its Triangle Run between Vancouver, Victoria and Seattle and coastal service *Princess* ferries. They were mostly not new, having been built before the First War between 1903 and 1910, so Thornton imagined he could have built new, faster and better ships to advantageously compete in those waters, as well as for cruises up to Alaska. Either line's ships were quite adequate to cover requirements. CN's intrusion in those markets "could succeed only in embarrassing without the compensation of profit" was a later assessment.

With the example of the successful *Lady* boats on the Atlantic, and satisfaction with their builders, Thornton's new ships were planned for the West Coast routes. With approval of his Board they were ordered from Cammell Laird & Co. in Birkenhead in early 1929. With the world-wide collapse of economies shortly after October 1929, for the CN they were close to a disaster. And Thornton had associated himself rather too closely with them, despite those three being but a smaller part of CN's operations.

Just to close out Sir Henry's career, although he had rescued the main focus of the CNR, expanded its services, engendered an enthusiasm among both management and line employees for their unified new company, he had also created enemies and dissenters. Despite profitability of the main rail operations, there was the never-resolved crippling burden of capital indebtedness inherited from the nationalized roads, and unprofitable branch lines that, politically, could hardly be just abandoned. He instituted radio broadcasting for his train passengers. It was the precursor to the CBC, yet local MPs in the Maritimes (including a relative of author Fraser McKee's, Senator Thomas Cantley) and regional newspapers fanned local complaints of lack of commitment to that area. He "lived large", gave highly visible parties and traveled overseas. The purpose of those trips was claimed as promotional and that claim was indeed true. But by 1931 and 1932 they were drawing additional criticism. His status was not helped by a divorce from his first wife. In the 1920s divorce was possible but heavily frowned upon. Despite the onslaught of the depression, he still continuously and vocally espoused expansion, competition with his rival wherever it could be met, and increased colonial settlement. With everyone else struggling, it was no longer popular or supportive by taxpayers and thus Governments.

With a change in government from King's Liberals, and CNR supporters, came R.B. Bennett's Conservatives, who tended toward the CPR's well run big business. The Government's subsidies of the CN's debt and other fringe and losing enterprises led to a Parliamentary Commission hearing, which produced a highly critical assessment of the Government's railway and its aims. So that body arranged to have Thornton relieved of his job as President in

1932. Technically he resigned as of August 1st, 1932 as was released publicly, but not only was he dismissed by Dr. Manion, the Minister of Railways, but left with no pension for all he had done for both the road and the country's development. He received only a one time retirement grant of $50,000, barely enough to cover his outstanding expenses. A broken man and by then ill, he returned to the States, and died in New York at only 63, ostensibly of cancer, in less than two years, on March 14th, 1934. He is buried at Newtown, Pennsylvania, the funeral covered extensively and sympathetically in the Canadian and US press. The week before he died he had been invited to return to Montreal to a dinner sponsored by his old and constant supporters, the railway unions and their General Chairman. His first wife, Virginia Blain, was buried beside him when she died in 1944. They had one son, James.

Sir Henry Worth Thornton - an unknown Canadian indeed.

CHAPTER TWO

Great Ships, Wrong Timing

There is a tide in the affairs of men which, taken at the flood, leads on to fortune;
Omitted, all the voyage of their life is bound in shallows and in miseries.
On such a full sea are we now afloat, and we must take the current where it serves…

Shakespeare, 'Julius Caesar'
Act 4, Sc.3

WHEN THE CANADIAN NATIONAL STEAMSHIP SERVICE (the CNSS) ordered the three new passenger ships in early 1929 times were booming, the economy was buoyant, and Sir Henry Thornton was still determined to compete in all markets his railway reached. The CNSS already had had smaller ships on the west coast since at least 1910, serving towns up the B.C. coast. There were the five brand new larger passenger freighters of the *Lady* boat ships on the Atlantic. So this was not a new venture in ship owning and operating. In fact the CN stressed they were simply intending to resume their service on the Triangle Run between Vancouver-Victoria-Seattle cities they had given up in 1922.

The three ships cost more than $2,000,000 each, a total of some $6.5 million, a vast sum by the end of 1930 when they were being paid for. They were to be built by one of the world's premier shipbuilders, Cammell Laird and Company in Birkenhead, in business for 125 years. They were the builders of the satisfactory *Lady* boats in the previous two years, ordered in 1927. In retrospect, it would have been interesting to sit in the background of the Railway's Board meeting when this new and very costly project was approved, and listened to Sir Henry's enthusiastic persuasiveness. Now we can see clearly that it would be dubious they would ever cover their costs and return a profit in competition with the CPR's services over the same routes. But Sir Henry carried the day with his people and the venture forged ahead.

Later there were claims that "the Easterners" had never consulted with those on the job already in B.C. as to appropriate ships for that trade. And one note says that Cammell Laird, when the ships' planned use was discussed, had some doubts these ordered ships would be suitable for the service intended but were overruled. The CN sent engineers to Birkenhead to represent their interests. They were designed by the experienced firm of A.T. Wall & Co. of Liverpool.

All three were almost identical, with only small variations in fittings. Each was 385 feet overall, with a 57 foot beam, and drew about 16½ feet or more depending on loading. They were of 6,893 gross registered tons (grt), usually referred to as 7,000-ton ships compared to the *Lady* boat's 7,900 and 8,100 grt. The CN and Wall opted for the latest in oil fuelled engine technology, with the most modern Parson's 3-stage single reduction geared turbines on two shafts. Steam was supplied by six Yarrow water tube five drum boilers giving 14,500 shaft horsepower at 22½ knots, although *Prince Robert* achieved 23¼ on her trials. It was called "An engineering advance." There were also two Scotch auxiliary boilers for other services. They had a range of 6,000 miles at economical speeds of just over 12 knots, but closer to 3,000 miles at their designed operating speed of 20 knots. This speed advantage was to be one of their big advantages over the slower CPR ships, although that was more costly in fuel. At that speed they burned just under 1.6 barrels of oil per mile. For some unknown reason the *Robert*, the last built, had a fuel capacity of 70 tons more than her sisters. Being essentially a passenger ship, there was considerable attention paid to water-tight bulkheads, carried up to the main deck (unlike the *Titanic!*) and to fire prevention and control. Lack of adequate fresh water was always a problem and the Masters made a point of taking it on by hose whenever in port for any time. When the Navy took over the ships in 1939 new evaporators were installed to provide a better self-contained supply.

Shell doors were set in along the midships at each deck to accommodate the heights of various jetties on the west coast, and there was a central elevator carrying two cars and small freight dollies to move them into the holds, a new concept. The story of their flared bows on occasion removing roofs of some jetty buildings when they approached at too sharp an angle is a post-war fabrication, as they were rather wall-sided with little flare. Their total freight, baggage and car capacity was about 51,800 cubic feet in a forward hold, tween decks and refrigerated space, making them useful for freight carriage as well.

In accommodation each ship had two special deluxe suites with bedroom, sitting room, a bathroom and luggage room. There were 20 "parlour" rooms with bathrooms, finished in polished exotic woods, and 20 rooms with a bed, a berth and a shower. There was further accommodation for 334 First Class passengers in other smaller cabins on the upper, bridge and promenade deck, with a full width large observation room at the forward end of the latter. Also there were 70 small two-berth Third Class cabins, and seating for 1,500 day passengers in lounges. A dining room to seat 280 at a sitting was on the main deck with tables for 2, 4, 6 and more. Afternoon tea and a late evening snack were advertised in their brochures. Separate messes, a lounge and smoking room were provided for the ships' officers, and others for the crew who were berthed forward.

Cammell Laird noted a bit sourly in their company magazine some 30 years later that the crews on commissioning were paid three times that for local British merchant seamen. There was a beauty and barber shop, a sales store and other passenger amenities to make their voyages enjoyable and memorable. One ship's public room decoration was "in the Spanish style," the other two in differing Old English decor. The Puget Sound Maritime Historical Society Journal didn't say which ship had which design, although photos of *Prince Henry* show a fireplace with shotguns on the wall over a mantlepiece, armchairs in front, and a carpet which could be removed for dancing. It had rather the air of a good English club.

As for costs, *Prince Robert* cost the CNSS $2,187,789, including some $10,300 in later improvements during the 1930s for such as extra berth ladders and cafeteria furnishings. Initial furnishings were over $383,500, and delivery charges for crew and Panama Canal fees were $86,400. Payments for each ship were to be made in five equal instalments, for *Robert* in July and December 1929, and March, April and October 1930. *Prince David* cost $2,144,387. *Robert's* daily operating costs were $1,372 with passengers (excluding passenger victualling), and at an economical operating speed of 16½ knots. And all of this was in early 1930, with the depression hitting the CN as everyone else.

Despite the Royal soubriquets, according to the CNR's historian in 1969, the ships were named for CNSS senior officers: *Robert* for the General Manager of CNSS Robert B. Teakle, *David* for CNSS Vice-President David E. Galloway and *Prince Henry* of course for Thornton himself. Other maritime historians suggest *Robert* was named for CNR Vice-President Robert C. Vaughan and *David* for David B. Hanna, Thornton's predecessor as President. One would assume the former is correct, but Board minutes do not seem to exist to confirm it.

In Service

Prince Henry, considered the trio's flagship, was launched on 17 January 1930. She was christened by Miss Ishbel MacDonald, the daughter of the then British Prime Minister Ramsay MacDonald, indicating Thornton's connections still existing over there. The *Henry* left Liverpool on 27 May, sailing via the Azores and Panama Canal and arrived in Victoria on 3 June after a 9,000-mile delivery voyage to quite a grand reception, dressed overall with her signal flags. As planned by now, *Prince Henry* was to be employed for cruises to Skagway, Alaska and back, while the other two eventually re-established the CNSS's Triangle Run services between Vancouver, Victoria and Seattle. The *Henry* was to provide a backup for the other two during the winter months when not employed cruising.

Prince Henry on B.C. coast in early 1930s   CN Steamships photo

After receptions and a dinner for 180 invited guests, she departed on a first cruise to Alaska on 3 July from Vancouver, under Captain A.J. Gilbert. The CNSS's Pacific Fleet Commodore, Captain Dan Donald was along as well. Four bridal couples on honeymoon trips were given commemorative silver vases. It was understood to be an indication of the CN commitment to enhanced services on the coast – "A luxurious new class of Prince ships that were to revolutionize the company's operations in the southwest corner of the Province." That was in itself true, but it couldn't last.

Prince Robert off an Alaskan glacier 1930s CN Steamships photo

Prince David was launched on 12 February 1930, apparently christened by some lesser noted personage, and sailed for Canada on 10 July, arriving on 3 August. At once, under Captain Henry Nedden, she was put on the Triangle Run on the 12th, alternating with one of the CN's older ships. The whole plan was not helped by a disastrous fire in the CNR's sheds on their pier on 10 August, forcing their ships to make use of the CPR's facilities nearby for the time being. It was an example of local cooperation, even if the senior executives in the East were battling each other.

The third ship, *Prince Robert*, was launched on 4 April 1930, sailed under Captain S. F. Cameron in late July, had some engine problems which required a return to Cammell Laird's for quick

Movies on board for passengers CN Steamships photo

repairs, and then went to Halifax. She was too late in the season to make Victoria and take her place with *Prince David* as intended. From Halifax she went to Boston, she then made three cruises of 14 days each to Bermuda, Jamaica and Havana and return, continuing similar journeys during the winter. For these she would leave Boston at 2 p.m. Then *Robert* was chartered in the spring of 1931 to go to Buenos Aires for the British Empire Trade Fair, opened by the Prince of Wales to encourage trade between South America and Britain and other Commonwealth Dominions. She carried delegations from the Canadian Chamber of Commerce and the Canadian Manufacturers Association, a first visit for a Canadian flagged cruise ship to that part of South America. On return to Canada, on 15 April she left Halifax for the West Coast, carrying a modest number of tourists for the voyage. She arrived in Vancouver on 8 May, and joined *Prince David* as the alternate on the Triangle

Prince Henry entering Vancouver. Note open cargo door above lower rubbing strake. Courtesy of Maritime Museum of B.C.

Run, relieving *Prince Henry* who had filled in on completion of her Alaskan cruises in the fall of 1930.

As an example, *David* would depart Seattle at 1:00 a.m., reach Victoria at 7 a.m., depart at 8:30 for Vancouver; return to Victoria by 5:45, and leave for Seattle at 7:00 p.m., arriving at 10:30 p.m. It was a strenuous schedule, and in competition with the CP's ships, who, due to their somewhat slower speeds, omitted the Vancouver-Victoria extra passage – a selling point for CN.

Then the reduced demands for space on both the Triangle routes and Alaskan cruises brought on by the depression began to take effect. In 1931, the *Henry* alternated between Triangle Runs and Alaskan cruises in the summer. She struck a log in March and spent 15 days having propellers repaired. On 21 November she left the West Coast, her services surplus to traffic requirements, never

CANADIAN NATIONAL STEAMSHIPS

ALASKA SAILINGS ⟋ SEASON 1930

S.S. "PRINCE RUPERT" ⟋ S.S. "PRINCE GEORGE"
S.S. "PRINCE HENRY"

No. of Sail-ings	NORTHBOUND			STEAMER	SOUTHBOUND		
	Leave Vancouver 10.00 p.m.	Leave Prince Rupert 2.30 p.m.	Arrive Skagway *7.00 a.m.		Leave Skagway *7.00 p.m.	Arrive Prince Rupert 7.00 a.m.	Arrive Vancouver 9.30 a.m.
1	June 9	June 11	June 13	......Prince George......	June 14	June 16	June 18
2	June 16	June 18	June 20	......Prince Rupert......	June 21	June 23	June 25
3	June 23	June 25	June 27	......Prince George......	June 28	June 30	July 2
4	June 30	July 2	July 4	......Prince Rupert......	July 5	July 7	July 9
5	July 3	July 5	July 7	......Prince Henry.......	July 7	July 9	July 10
6	July 7	July 9	July 11	......Prince George......	July 12	July 14	July 16
7	July 10	July 12	July 14	......Prince Henry.......	July 14	July 16	July 17
8	July 14	July 16	July 18	......Prince Rupert......	July 19	July 21	July 23
9	July 17	July 19	July 21	......Prince Henry.......	July 21	July 23	July 24
10	July 21	July 23	July 25	......Prince George......	July 26	July 28	July 30
11	July 24	July 26	July 28	......Prince Henry.......	July 28	July 30	July 31
12	July 28	July 30	Aug. 1	......Prince Rupert......	Aug. 2	Aug. 4	Aug. 6
13	July 31	Aug. 2	Aug. 4	......Prince Henry.......	Aug. 4	Aug. 6	Aug. 7
14	Aug. 4	Aug. 6	Aug. 8	......Prince George......	Aug. 9	Aug. 11	Aug. 13
15	Aug. 7	Aug. 9	Aug. 11	......Prince Henry.......	Aug. 11	Aug. 13	Aug. 14
16	Aug. 11	Aug. 13	Aug. 15	......Prince Rupert......	Aug. 16	Aug. 18	Aug. 20
17	Aug. 14	Aug. 16	Aug. 18	......Prince Henry.......	Aug. 18	Aug. 20	Aug. 21
18	Aug. 18	Aug. 20	Aug. 22	......Prince George......	Aug. 23	Aug. 25	Aug. 27
19	Aug. 21	Aug. 23	Aug. 25	......Prince Henry.......	Aug. 25	Aug. 27	Aug. 28
20	Aug. 25	Aug. 27	Aug. 29	......Prince Rupert......	Aug. 30	Sept. 1	Sept. 3

*Ship's Time. Alaska Time is one hour slower.

The times and dates of arrival and departure are subject to tidal and other conditions.

The fare from VANCOUVER, B.C. to SKAGWAY, ALASKA and RETURN

NINETY DOLLARS ($90.00)

And upwards according to accommodation occupied.

ALL OUTSIDE ROOMS.

Detailed information may be obtained from any Canadian National Passenger Representative.

Fare includes meals and stateroom accommodation en route, but not on board steamer while in port at Skagway.

Fares quoted as applying between Vancouver and Skagway, will also apply for passengers embarking at Prince Rupert, B.C., and proceeding from there to Skagway, returning to Prince Rupert or Vancouver, or vice versa.

Prince Henry sailing schedule 1930 CN Steamships photo

to return in her civilian guise. She carried passengers on the 23-day cruise to Halifax, then made 24 round trips Boston to Bermuda and three Boston to Havana, being laid up at Halifax periodically when not required. Even on those trips there was competition with her own cohorts, the CNSS's larger *Lady* boats, that had the advantage of carrying considerably more commercial freight, bananas in particular, from the West Indies to Halifax and Montreal.

In 1936 *Prince Henry* was chartered to National Pleasure Tours of New York City for one tour from New York, Panama Canal,

TSS North Star daily program Labrador cruise 1939 Author's collection

TSS North Star ex Prince Henry at Montreal 1938 Author's collection

Skagway Alaska and return via Hawaii, by 31 July. Returned to Halifax, she was laid up there until 1937. By this time CN was searching for ways to either unload the less than profitable *Prince* ships, or at least find ways to make added revenue from them. Clarke Steamship Co. Ltd. of Quebec City approached CNSS to charter *Prince Henry* for their cruising services. Clarke had smaller ships serving the St. Lawrence River and Gulf communities for local pleasure cruises and light freight traffic out to Newfoundland but needed a somewhat larger ship. The *Henry* fitted their requirements. She was taken to a local shipyard, painted the Clarke's white overall with four narrow light blue bands on her funnel replacing the CNSS's blue white and red. They rènamed her *North Star*. That name had an old Canadian connection as *North Star* was the sole surviving ship of Captain William Belcher's disastrous search in the Arctic for the lost ships of Sir John Franklin in 1852.

That summer *North Star* made cruises around the Gulf, up the Saguenay, around Prince Edward Island and Nova Scotia. Author

TSS North Star on board postcard July 1938 Author's collection

Fraser McKee made a few quarters taking bags ashore at Pictou, N.S. when she called – a rather large vessel for that narrow harbour, as he recalls much mud stirred up as the vessel laboriously turned in the upper reaches. In December 1938 Clarke bought the ship, with the CNSS holding the mortgage, and with a provision that she could not be re-sold to anyone without the CNR's agreement. By this time there were other bidders starting to show an interest in the ships as the effects of the depression eased. Cruises started alternately at Montreal and New York, with calls at Botwood in western Newfoundland as well. In the winters of 1937 and '38 she filled in with cruises from Miami to the West Indies. In the early summer of 1939 there was a long cruise from New York to the west coast and return. But a planned series from New York to Miami and beyond in September were cancelled. The war in Europe had begun, and there were other and prearranged calls on the *Princes*.

Meanwhile *Prince David*, operating on the Triangle Run, proved to be the unlucky ship of the trio. On 31 July 1931, she was run onto the beach at Port Townsend at the American entrance to Puget Sound in heavy fog. There were no casualties, and passengers were all taken off by a smaller ferry, and no doubt to the CN's embarrassment, transferred to the CP's *Princess Kathleen*. They were returned to Victoria to continue their voyage – if they still wished – to Seattle in *David's* alternate by then, *Prince Robert*. *Prince David* later floated off with the rising tide, assisted by a tug. The Master had his license suspended for several months for going too fast in fog and the repairs cost CN almost $90,000.

CANADIAN NATIONAL STEAMSHIPS

PRINTED IN CANADA

14 Day Cruise – Twin-Screw Steamer "Prince Robert"
Boston – Bermuda – Jamaica – Havana – Boston

Prince Robert on board post card Courtesy John Roue, Ottawa

As mentioned before, by September, 1931 there was obviously not enough traffic on the route to warrant both CN and CP's ships, so the CN suspended their Triangle Run on 15 September, and it was never re-established by them. The building underway since 1930 as a large harbour hotel in Vancouver, to have been called reportedly The Thornton Hotel, was suspended, partly completed. It was not finished until the late 1930s. The *David* lay idle

Three Princes Armed

at Victoria until 12 December, 1931 when she sailed with cruise tourists for Halifax to join the *Prince Henry* and *Prince Robert*. From January 1932 the *Prince David* found employment on four cruises between Boston, Bermuda and the Caribbean.

Prince David aground on a Bermuda reef 1932 Author's collection

However, continuing her saga of too close affiliation with the land, on the second cruise, on 12 March 1932, she went seriously aground on a reef, the Northeast Breaker, near Hamilton Harbour at Bermuda. A large gash was torn in her hull toward the stern, and again although there were no casualties, at first it was assumed she would be a total loss. D.B. Hanna, appearing later before a Senate Committee on railway expenses commented that he had felt "This would at least relieve the CN of that white elephant." Not all CN's management had Sir Henry's earlier enthusiasm. But with some effort the ship was refloated a month and a half later on 25 April with the aid of the tug *Killoric*. Temporarily patched, she was towed to Halifax Shipyards for repairs, arriving on 5 May. The total cost of towing and repairs was $1,058,204 most of which was recovered through insurance.

After the repairs, *David* continued cruising in 1934, with 43 Miami to Nassau cruises, departing on Monday, Wednesday and Friday, with passengers in hotels at each end for a night or two. But this lasted only for that one season, as again the ship proved too large for the traffic available. A planned series of summer cruises from Boston up to the Saguenay and Quebec were cancelled when it was assessed that there was already too much competition on that route, part of it from the CP's ships. The *David* was laid up for almost a year, then, like the *Prince Henry*, chartered to National Pleasure Cruises for one trip from New York to the Panama and Alaska. Considering this was in 1936, there were enough takers even at a cost of $2,450 for the deluxe cabins, and $595 for single passengers. Looking at her record, one gets the impression these ships, with the slow reacting turbine engines when moved from "Ahead" to "Astern", were difficult to handle in restricted locations. There are several reports in their files in the Archives of damage caused when striking piers between 1934 and 1937, and another grounding when one was being moved by a tug at Bermuda in 1936 and the tow wire broke. The engines gave a good speed, but turbines had expensive disadvantages compared to steam triple expansion and diesel engines. In the fall of 1937 the *David* also was laid up at Halifax pending possible sale.

The *Prince Robert* on the other hand led a much more satisfactory career, and in fact was the only ship of the three to return a small profit to CNSS. After the demise of the CN's Triangle service, she too went around to Halifax in the fall of 1931, undertook Boston to West Indies cruises, then returned to the West Coast for Alaska cruises in 1932. But at the end of that season the demand ran out, and she was laid up there until 1935, when *Robert* made four eleven-day cruises to Alaska and shorter ones up to Powell River and elsewhere on the B.C. coast. This continued each summer, with usually winter lay-ups. In the spring of 1939 with considerable pomp and attention she carried King George VI and Queen Elizabeth from Victoria to Vancouver to continue their triumphal pre-war journey, the ship setting a speed record for the crossing. Then more Alaska cruises followed. But for her too war loomed, and like her sisters, a naval career for six strenuous years lay ahead.

Sale Possibilities and Preparations For War

In 1935, with the *Princes'* operations mostly a losing operation - Hanna's "white elephants" – and at best underused, the CNR's Board noted that "It is the policy of the Trustees to dispose of these vessels by sale if reasonable terms can be secured." By 1937 at least one Greek firm was interested in them for cruising, probably in the Mediterranean. Their terms suggested were lower than hoped for by CN who hesitated to bite at the offer. As well the Navy, according to Vice-Admiral Percy Nelles (in his records, commenting in September 1942), opposed any sale outside Canada in a representation to the Transport Minister. The Navy already considered the three would be adaptable as Armed Merchant Cruisers if armament could be located. Although not costing anything at that time, it was one sign of preparedness for war in the face of the later usual accusations of the Services being completely unprepared. And Nelles knew there were suitable guns stored in Canada, although the property of the British Admiralty.

The matter of sale arose again in 1938 with Turkish interest in buying the ships for about $750,000 to $800,000 which the CNR would no doubt have accepted. And again the Chief of the Naval Staff, supported by the Honorary Naval Advisory Committee (of

Reserve Officers, some of whom had connections in Ottawa), opposed any sale. This quiet application of pressure is confirmed by CNR officials who simply noted that "they had been prevented from selling them." The Navy appreciated their good speed, and while uneconomical for their then owners, this would make them useful naval vessels.

With the two vessels at Halifax and *Prince Robert* on the west coast and Canada about to join Britain in declaring war on Germany in early September, the Navy in effect reserved the three for possible use. On 9 September 1939 the Admiralty were asked if guns and anti-submarine equipment from their stores in Canada at Montreal and Esquimalt could be provided for the RCN to mount on the *Princes*. The Admiralty replied that they could release two gun outfits, but thought a third should be retained in case a larger or more powerful liner might become available. The Navy, through civilian Ministries, opened discussions with the CNR re acquiring at least the two *Princes* still in CN hands, *David* at Halifax and *Robert*. As well Clarke Steamship Co. was told that the CN intended to apply the term in the sale contract that allowed it to re-acquire *North Star* ex-*Prince Henry*. At first it was thought the ships would all be taken over on a lease or charter. But in a letter from R.K. Smith of the Government's Marine Services to Rear Admiral Nelles, he recommended that due to the substantial alterations that would be required, the Navy buy the ships, at an offered $750,000. It all seems a bit academic, since it was in reality simply a transfer of them from a wholly owned Government subsidiary to the Navy, but it kept the books straight, and provided the financially pressed CNR with a substantial bookkeeping sum.

Pending the financial agreement, still very much not settled, arrangements were put in hand to acquire the two CN vessels, with the Navy again pressing the Admiralty for a third set of gunnery equipment for the *Henry*. It was not until 8 January 1940 that they agreed, that the guns and equipment could be taken from the Montreal store, from which several of their own merchantmen then in the Montreal area were being armed.

There was a long and contentious exchange between the Navy, the Department of Defence, the CNR and Clarke Steamship Co., and no agreement was reached on the final price until the spring of 1940. The first two ships, *David* and *Robert*, went into dockyard hands in the second week of February, *Robert* at Burrard Dry Dock Co. in Vancouver and *David* at Halifax Shipyard to convert them to AMCs. *Robert* was purchased for $738,310 and *David* for $739,663. It was not until the beginning of May that negotiations could be concluded for *North Star*, by this time HMCS *Prince Henry*, and at a cost of $638,224. For her conversion she went to Canadian Vickers Ltd. in Montreal.

Thus the three CNR millstones embarked on a new and at least for the country in general far more valuable enterprise.

CHAPTER THREE
1940 – 1943

Some Early Success and Much Patrolling

"A kingdom for a stage, princes to act, and monarchs to behold the swelling scene"

Shakespeare - *"Henry V"* Chorus 1.1

THE STORY OF THE ROYAL CANADIAN NAVY in World War II has by now been thoroughly researched and documented by qualified historians. The first two volumes of the official history have been published. There have been books on individual ships such as *Haida*, *Swansea*, *Uganda* and *Nabob*. Numerous autobiographies have appeared, some by those in command such as the two volumes from Admiral Brock, and some from some sailors who fought the war from their action stations and mess decks of the smaller ships. So there is little coverage that remains. This book chooses in continuation to shed some light on three RCN ships whose service history has been referred to in numerous volumes but never treated as a complete story. The authors make no claim to significant new research. Rather they have gathered together much that has already been written and published. In particular, a generous portion of what is contained in these next four chapters has been drawn from a paper written in Department of National Defence (DHist. now Directorate of History & Heritage) by Malcolm Macleod in October 1965 titled "The Prince Ships 1940-1945."

These three ships are frequently referred to as Armed Merchant Cruisers (AMC). This designation was apt for *Prince Robert* which spent the war in that role. *Prince Robert* was identified as an Auxiliary Anti-Aircraft Ship after being re-armed with ten 4-inch high angle, low angle (HA/LA) guns in 1943. But for *Prince David* and *Prince Henry* their service as AMCs ended when they were converted to Infantry Landing Ships in preparation for duty in landing soldiers during the invasion of Normandy and of southern France. They were officially designated Landing Ship Infantry (Medium).

Merchant ships have been converted for service in war since the beginning of action at sea. Those conversions have resulted in many uses. In both world wars the Germans developed ships primarily for use as commerce raiders. In World War 1 eighteen identified ships were armed by Germany. Some had weapons hidden behind false bulkheads so that they would appear to be innocent ships approaching under a false flag. Their successes varied. Many were sunk but others such as *Kronprinz Wilhelm* sank 15 ships in the early days of WWI before having to surrender in an American port. Also in WWI, Count Felix von Luckner in the armed sailing ship *Seadler* made a name for himself before being wrecked in the south Pacific. In both world wars German naval planners placed destruction of Great Britain's merchant fleet as a high priority.

In WWII the German raider *Kormoran* sank the Royal Australian Navy cruiser HMAS *Sydney* in a battle off the west coast of Australia in an engagement in which she herself was sunk. *Kormoran* was one of 11 ships that the Germans converted in WWII. Another German raider, the *Atlantis*, sank 22 ships totaling over 145,000 tons before being sunk by HMS *Devonshire* in November 1941. Some raiders like these had been purpose built.

They had reinforced decks with the intent of supporting guns in time of war. The weapons that were added normally consisted of 5.9-inch guns and some torpedo tubes, along with antiaircraft and anti-personnel weapons. Some had one or two Arado AR-196 seaplanes for searching out potential targets. These were lifted from the hold and launched and recovered by a boom or crane. The raiders also had extra spaces to accommodate prisoners taken from ships that they had sunk.

The British had success with decoy ships during WWI. From July 1915 until August 1917 decoy ships (known as "Q" ships) were used to entice U-boats to surface after the decoy pretended to abandon ship. At that time asdic (now called sonar) was in its infancy for underwater detecting. Once the U-boat was surfaced the decoy's guns were exposed and the submarine was an easy target. Eleven U-boats were destroyed before the Germans exercised exceptional caution to avoid being caught on the surface.

The Germans also converted ships to act as floating supply bases for their battleship commerce raiders. The *Altmark* was the 12,000-ton support ship for the *Graf Spee*. She had taken on board all the merchant prisoners from ships sunk by *Graf Spee*. A Royal Navy boarding party rescued the prisoners and found that *Altmark* was in fact armed with heavy and light machine guns. These hardly qualified *Altmark* as an Armed Merchant Cruiser but does show the variety of service by armed merchant type ships during wartime.

In WWI Britain converted 62 ships as AMC. Of these 15 were lost to all causes in the first two years of the war. It is difficult to assess their value from this distance. If an appreciation was ever done by the Admiralty such has not been available to this book. A recent book by Richard Osborne concludes that they were of dubious value. The ex-Cunard liner HMS *Carmania* engaged the Hamburg Sud Amerik's *Cap Trafalgar* off Trinidad and sank the German, which unfortunately for the Germans was disguised as *Carmania* herself. These converted liners were essentially of little value as fighting ships. They lacked armour protection, modern guns and gun direction equipment, but differed from Q ships in that their guns were not hidden.

In the early days of the WWII Britain was hard pressed to have all the ships necessary to fulfill the many and varied duties. One such duty was the Northern Patrol. This was the area of northern exits to the Atlantic between the Faroes Islands and Iceland as well as the Denmark Strait. The duties of ships on this patrol were to intercept German blockade runners as well as to watch for German heavy warships trying to pass through. In 1940 fully half the British fleet of AMC were assigned to this patrol.

The Royal Navy viewed the AMC from a different perspective. Admiral Erich Raeder, the head of the German navy, was building battleships and pocket battleships. In the 1930s the British Admiralty's main concern was not U-Boats but heavily armed raiders (eg *Scharnhorst* and *Gneisnau)* and countering them with rather too few cruisers due to the 1922 and 1930 naval treaties. Critical to Great Britain in both world wars was her lifeline of maritime commercial traffic. Her lack of self-sufficiency and her wide spread empire required an enormous traffic by sea, and these ships were a principal target of her enemies. Protection of convoys and sea-lanes was vital to maintain the safe return of goods laden ships. Great Britain had a large fleet of liners and other large ships suitable for conversion to AMC and use in the convoy protection role. Although with little value as anti-submarine vessels these large ships might have deterred German ships of a similar size from doing severe damage.

There was one classic engagement of an AMC and the German pocket battleship *Admiral Scheer* on 5 November 1940. HMS *Jervis Bay,* under the command of Captain E.S. Fogerty Fegen stood up against the *Admiral Scheer* in a fight that could only have one outcome. It was seven ancient 6-inch guns against modern 11-inch guns with far greater range and with modern fire control equipment.

While convoy HX 84 scattered *Jervis Bay* was beaten to a sinking wreck. Fegen was awarded the Victoria Cross. However all but five of the 37 ships he protected were able to escape the German large caliber guns.

The German ships were without overseas repair facilities and could risk little serious damage. When the large German warships were no longer the main threat to convoys and the submarines became the principal weapon of the enemy, the AMC were withdrawn from convoy protection duties. Many of these ships then became troop carriers. Many larger ships were provided with considerable armament for self protection.

In November of 1940 the AMC HMS *Rawalpindi* was on the Northern Patrol when two German battle cruisers were conducting an operation in the Iceland-Faroes Channel to disrupt British shipping. *Rawalpindi* was sighted by *Scharnhorst*, who began firing when at 8,000 yards. The British ship achieved one hit on the German but within 14 minutes she was destroyed. The AMC fleet did continue as convoy escorts even though Winston Churchill when still First Lord of the Admiralty questioned whether they were essential given their expense. By February of 1940 Captain Roskill reports that "ten were allocated to the Freetown Escort Force, four to the Halifax Escort Force, some twenty to the Northern Patrol and the remaining dozen were divided between the Mediterranean, Pacific and Indian Oceans."

When war began in September 1939 many German merchant ships were in ports around the world. Preventing them from getting back to Germany with their valuable cargoes or even capturing them were additional duties that an AMC could well achieve. It is obvious from all the above that the principal adversaries in both world wars had definite uses for the AMC within the broad scope of their warfighting plans. We then might ask as to Canada's concept of employment for the three *Prince* ships.

At the outbreak of war in 1939 the Royal Canadian Navy

consisted of just a handful of destroyers and minesweepers. One of the first responses at Naval Service Headquarters was to survey the possible available Canadian ships of all sizes that might be of some use. Over a period of time a large number of vessels were acquired by requisition, charter or purchase. Inter alia these included yachts, former RCMP vessels, Norwegian whale boats (that escaped when Norway was invaded and were fitted as auxiliary minesweepers), fishing vessels, tugs and other miscellaneous craft. One has only to look at David Freeman's book "Canadian Warship Names" to see the multitude of vessels needed for the many duties of a wartime navy.

The largest of these acquisitions were the three *Prince* ships. Whether the planners in Ottawa had a precise vision as to the utility of the *Princes* is doubtful. Tucker says that naval staff recommended that they should be used to supplement available destroyers in providing protection against the anticipated surface raiders. With the Royal Navy pressing her liners into service as AMCs the example for the RCN existed. On the outbreak of WWII Canada had converted two of the British liners into AMCs. These were *Letitia* and *Rajputana*. The latter ship was converted by Yarrows on the west coast in 1939 but was lost in April 1941. A desk from her days as a liner is still in use by the Base Commander at Canadian Forces Base Esquimalt. With this conversion experience the RCN saw the possibility of some useful service for this type of ship as long as six inch guns could be provided from British stocks.

Robert was on the west coast and *David* and *Henry* on the east coast at the time they were acquired. Conversion of the three ships took place starting in February 1940 for the *David* and *Robert* and in May for the *Henry*, with design plans by German and Milne of Montreal. *David's* work was assigned to Halifax Shipyards, and *Robert's* to Burrard Dry Dock, Vancouver. *Henry* was undertaken by Canadian Vickers in Montreal. On commissioning each ship was assigned a pennant number: *Prince Robert* was F56, *Prince Henry* was F70 and *Prince David* was F89.

Prince Robert had been a much more active ship before its acquisition and as a result was in generally good condition. Although *Henry* had been cruising for Clark Steamship Line, *David* had been layed up for some time and required much more work on hull and machinery. These conversions were not the carefully planned and executed engineering tasks of today. The work was done in haste to meet the demands of the navy. The contractor, German & Milne, later said that the naval Constructor simply walked about *Henry* with a piece of chalk marking bulkheads to be cut away and hatches to be cut in the decks for the passing of shells to the guns. The end result was to give the ships the silhouette of a light cruiser, perhaps a *Hawkins* Class. This meant cutting off the top decks and constructing a new superstructure and bridge. Two single six inch guns were superimposed forward of the bridge (designated as "A" and "B") and two more in the aft portion of the ship (designated "X" and "Y"). Two three-inch guns were fitted on the upper deck amidships plus some 50 caliber machine guns. Two depth charge chutes were added at the stern although there was no asdic set on board used to detect a submarine. Sets were in very short supply and some intended for Canadian ships were lost when their freighter was sunk. Sets were installed at a later refit.

In 1988 Lieutenant G.R. (Bill) Johnson, RCNVR published a 23 page outline of the history of the *Prince Robert*. Bill had served in *Robert* as the Radar Officer and he had excellent talent as an artist. In his description of the main armament he noted that they were "up to 45 years old, without any semblance of range and fire control equipment." They had been manufactured as early as 1896 for the *King Edward* class battleships, (known as the Wobbly Eight) and were obsolete before WWI. Bill further described their training which "was sluggish and at times was assisted by a crew hauling lines attached to the gun muzzles." He generously noted that "the 3 inch guns were much more modern, being of 1916 vintage."

The Executive Officer of Prince Robert when that ship went to the Aleutians was Commander O.C.S. "Long Robbie" Robertson. He was quoted in Salty Dips Volume 3 on this subject. He said "We had 1906 guns with a central pivot mounting. We couldn't train them by crank and gears, they were rusted in. When you wanted to train, you put a couple of men on the barrel and pushed it around to get the training gear working." Malcolm Macleod in the 1965 NDHQ paper states that "It was not true that the guns in the *Prince* ships had been cast during the Boer War, and that the barrels were in imminent danger of bursting during firing, This rumour was prevalent in the RCN at the time." But the fact remains that the guns were obsolete and of limited use in combat.

"If these ships were initially intended for action against German blockade runners and supply ships for the surface ship raiders, they did have some advantages. They were large enough to carry a full complement of gunners. Their top speed of 22 knots was sufficient to overtake most German merchant ships. And their range of 7,500 miles gave them the advantage of staying at sea for extended operations. But these advantages in no way compensated for their shortcomings in a gun battle with German raiders. It is doubtful that the average sailor on board gave serious thoughts to these tactical limitations."

Internally much change was required. For a ship's company of approximately 250 accommodation was required, to be of the mess deck variety with cabins for the complement of 22 officers. As liners' watertight subdivisions were below naval requirements and so were extended somewhat. The large engine room spaces were thought by some to be potentially fatal if struck by a torpedo. Some deck stiffening was needed to support the guns.

In addition to the elderly armament, the ships had other disadvantages. Rear Admiral Frank Houghton commanded *Prince Robert* as a Captain from June of 1942 until December of the same year. Parts of his memoirs were printed in Salty Dips Volume 8 in 2002.

He stated "these craft tended to roll badly with a rapid and jerky motion, making them difficult and unsteady platforms. We carried no anti-aircraft armament as such and our radar was the oldest model of all – very rudimentary and not particularly trustworthy."

Throughout this narrative we will often refer to the *Prince* ships as "*Robert*" or "*Henry*." Those who served in them used that form of identity. Sailors served "on board" HMC ships but those with a strong sense of tradition always said "I was **in** the *Robert*." For many it was their first ship and also for many it was their first time near an ocean. For the RCN it was a golden opportunity to provide some senior officers with a Canadian sea command larger than a minesweeper. Not until late in the war when the navy acquired two cruisers and manned two light aircraft carriers were there sea commands for four stripe Captains except for the *Prince* ships. (Captain Harold Grant commanded the Royal Navy cruisers HMS *Diomede* and HMS *Enterprise* in 1943).

One of the sailors who commissioned the *Henry* remembers some of the internal arrangements. Norm Anderson joined in Victoria, B.C. and entered the navy as a Boy Seaman. He was trained in gunnery, and after the war was commissioned and ended as a Lieutenant Commander. He remembers that two decks down below the quarterdeck was a large mess deck for Leading Seamen and below. There was also a messdeck forward. It was an era when hammocks were used with hammock bars fitted to deck heads. Harold Moist in an interview many years later stated that all except the officers slung hammocks. The feeding system was of the "broadside" version. Each mess consisted of a number of sailors with a Leading Seaman or senior Able Seaman in charge. The "cook of the mess" went to the galley with a mess fanny and drew rations for the number in his mess. These were doled out by the senior hand. The cook of the mess later washed up and threw the "gash" overboard down a metal gash chute. This led to the sailor's ditty "Tinkle tinkle little spoon, knife and fork will follow soon." It was not until later that the RCN adopted the much more sensible cafeteria system of feeding. With the *Prince* ships the size of small liners cafeteria feeding would have been much more efficient, but naval ways are not easy to change.

Above the seaman's mess deck was a lounge where the sailors could relax. In that same area were Sick Bay, the office of the Master at Arms, (the ship's policeman), and some other office spaces. The Petty Officers' mess space was on the port side. The galley was amidships. The officers' cabins were forward along with the wardroom. Anderson's action station was on "B" gun and he does not recall any training problems. He states that his gun would train abaft the beam with no problems.

H.M.C.S. Prince Robert

With her condition in better shape than her two sisters *Prince Robert's* conversion took less time. She commissioned in Vancouver on 30 July 1940 under Commander Charles Taschereau Beard RCN. Beard was a graduate of the Naval College of Canada and was 50 years old when he took command. He had retired from the RCN shortly before the war but returned to duty at the outbreak. *Robert's* trials took place during August and the modifications that resulted were useful for the two later sisters. Trials were completed in early September. One serious problem arose when "B" gun's blast smashed the windows of the wheelhouse space behind that gun. All three ships then needed modifications to prevent this reoccurrence.

Although the captain of a warship usually sets the tone of the ship, sailors will confirm that a ship is a small steel box full of people interacting with one another. Among them will be at least one "character." For the *Robert* that one was "Dhobie" Hart. He was a Royal Navy deserter who joined after a blanket amnesty had been issued by the Admiralty and was on board officially to run the officer's laundry. He scorned rules, stole food from the galley, went ashore in an officer's uniform, caused the ship to delay sailing, was master of ceremonies at on board entertainment and was frequently before the Executive Officer charged with various offenses. Lieutenant-Commander G.B. Hope invariably stopped his leave for periods when the ship was at sea. His excuse was that Hart was instrumental in maintaining morale in the ship.

Retired Commander George MacFarlane had been a Leading Torpedoman in *Prince Robert* and many years later recalled clearly others on board. He remembered that in the summer of 1940 the West Coast did not have a lot of seamen available since they were mostly shipped off to East Coast ships. *Robert* commissioned with a lot of "hard cases." Some were veterans of the Spanish Civil War and others were, like Hart, pardoned deserters. According to MacFarlane, Commander Hope ran the ship. He had been in the Royal Navy until 1920. He had been hired to break a longshoreman's strike in San Francisco and was rumored to have been in Ireland during "the troubles of 1921." His rules were much like those of World War I of the Royal Navy and were not very much to the liking of his sailors. Even the junior officers were treated like RN Midshipmen of an earlier era. MacFarlane said he was "a vain, hard, competent officer, but perhaps the right man for the job given the makeup of the crew."

Retired Chief Gunner's Mate Doug Allen was a Boy Seaman on board. He remembers Petty Officer "Doc" Miles who was responsible for the Boys. Men like Miles, Chief ERA Lang and Petty Officer Harold Moist were the real strength of the ship. Moist was a pre-war Reservist from Winnipeg. He was 86 when interviewed in Victoria in 1999 but his memories were clear as ever. He had commissioned the ship and did not leave her until July 1945. He too recalls that the after mess was full of RCNR seamen who "were a rough and tough group of individualists." The forward mess was full of RCNVR with little or no experience. Moist felt that when she sailed south the ship was "totally unfit for any armed opposition."

John Maw had briefly joined the Canadian Army then the RCAF, before he was accepted as an Engineer Officer in the RCNVR. He joined *Prince Robert* in early 1942 to find competent engineering staff and equipment that was in good shape with a top speed of 24 knots when needed. He recalled one Engineer of the Watch who tried to sneak out or "blow a little soot" to clear the funnels. He actually sent up a large black cloud. The Captain on the bridge rang down "You are blowing black smoke!" Thinking it was just the Officer of the Watch he replied "What do you want, snowballs." He received the usual blast from the Captain.

Although naval planners had not constructed a long-term plan for the use of AMCs, it was apparent very early on that the German merchant ships then at sea were obvious targets. *Robert* was the only RCN AMC on the West Coast. One of the known Germans was the *Weser* in Manzanillo, Mexico, plus there were several others like *Hermonthis* further south. Captain Roskill in Appendix N to his War At Sea Volume 1 listed 39 German supply ships working with raiders and U–boats. These, added to another 22 captured ships used as supply ships to raiders, and to numerous German merchant ships hoping to run the blockade to a home port created numerous targets for the limited assets of Allied ships to seek out and destroy. Canadian ships played an early role in that task.

Prince Robert was far from being operationally ready and was over 2,000 miles from Manzanillo. A known German agent in Seattle was reporting ship movements. But through Vancouver newspaper connivance it was indicated that *Robert* was still in Vancouver although she had already sailed on 11 September 1940 with orders to intercept the *Weser*. The voyage south was overshadowed by the need to avoid being identified by other ships met en route. It resulted in two incidents. The first, for Canada had been at war with Italy since July, involved boarding a Philippines ship and taking its Italian engineer as a prisoner. The second was a minor fiasco when Commander Beard attempted to pass his prisoner off to a British ship, but the captain of the *Hoperidge* thought he was being attacked and threw his valuable confidential books over the side. Beard stated to the press later that the captain was a very peeved man when he found out who had stopped him.

Prince Robert arrived off Manzanillo on the 18th. Beard patrolled well clear of land during daylight hours and close to the harbour exit that he thought *Weser* would use after dark. He took great care to see that he remained outside Mexico's territorial waters, and entered precise positions in his ship's log after verification by himself and other officers. After one week of this tactic and on a night that Beard described as a bit foggy, the Captain was gratified to see a dark object moving in a seaward direction. Beard had placed his ship further inshore so that he was invisible against the high shore line behind him. As the other ship moved further out to sea Beard moved to cut off a possible retreat to the harbour. Beard soon was able to confirm that it was indeed the *Weser* that was attempting to escape.

In a press interview on return to Esquimalt Beard summarized the action and capture. As he closed the *Weser* he put a searchlight on her bridge, fired one starshell over the German, and one six inch shell ahead the German ship. He then put a searchlight to illuminate his own six-inch guns. He was close enough so that he was able to hail *Weser* from his bridge and order him to stop. He found out later that Captain Veit of the *Weser* thought at first that he was being stopped by a Mexican gunboat so did not rush to destroy his ship. Beard commented later that "It was almost too easy. We had no trouble at all." The German officers thought they were clear and some of them were about to toast to a safe get-away.

Prince Robert lowered the cutter with the boarding party under the command of the Executive Officer Lieutenant-Commander

Geoffrey Hope. In the party also were 22 men including Sub-Lieutenant Dundas, Warrant Officers Kincaid and Mathieson, Petty Officer Harold Moist and Able Seaman Cody. Expecting great difficulty getting to the deck of *Weser* the boarding party was delighted to discover the accommodation ladder still rigged due to the ship's secret departure, and they were able simply to climb on board. Beard gave full credit to Hope for his conduct of the boarding. Hope reported later that "the *Weser's* Chief Officer met me as I boarded and was a little stubborn so I shouldered him aside." Petty Officer Moist had his pistol on a lanyard but it slipped as he was boarding. Grabbing the barrel he had to knock a German on the head with the gun when he thought he was being opposed. It was noticed that the Germans had made preparations for setting their ship on fire but failed to do so because *Robert* did not give them time.

Crew members of the Weser being marched off to prisoner of war camp
Courtesy Naval and Military museum of Esquimalt

In 1999 Robert Dundas wrote his recollections of the boarding. His action station was a 3-inch gun that fired the starshell. He was then ordered to the boarding party. Once on deck he rushed to the bridge where he found the captain who spoke excellent English. He remembers the livestock that made a feast for the trailing sharks since it was considered to be inedible. And he recalled with pleasure the cold German beer he found in the fridge after being warned not to drink the ship's water. Dundas stayed on board to Esquimalt.

Prince Robert and Weser at Esquimalt   Courtesy Naval and Military Museum of Esquimalt

The boarders found 58 officers and men on the *Weser* plus a German shepherd dog later acquired by Sub-Lieutenant Dundas. Some of the Germans, particularly the officers, were cocky and arrogant but the diesel engineers and 15 German volunteers were retained on board by the prize crew in bringing the *Weser* back to Esquimalt. Lieutenant-Commander Hope commanded the prize crew. The remaining 43 Germans were taken on board *Prince Robert*. All the crew were later interned but were not treated as prisoners of war. Beard told the press some of the details. Some of the crew had only tropical clothing so were given some heavier clothing by men of the *Robert*. Beard said that the Germans expected harsher treatment, perhaps even execution, but were no trouble on the

Three Princes Armed

M. V. WESER—PRIZE OF WAR.

With a Canadian naval prize crew aboard, the North | Her capture by the Royal Canadian Navy's armed
rman Lloyd line's modern 10,000-ton motor-vessel | merchant cruiser Prince Robert, off the coast of Mexic
ser is proceeding to Esquimalt, the White Ensign | last night, was announced to-day.
the Empire's navies flying above her swastika flag. |

Weser in Vancouver   News photo believed to be from the Vancouver Province

homeward journey. *Prince Robert* escorted her prize into Esquimalt harbour on 4 October 1940 to a warm and triumphant 19th century welcome.

Weser was a 9,180 ton ship, 487 feet in length and with a top speed of 17 knots. Captain Roskill in Table "I" to his War At Sea listed her as a planned support ship for the German raider *Orion*. She carried a quantity of diesel oil, so that function may have been true. But her main cargo consisted of peat moss and coke and was of little value to a raider, or to Canada. Commander Beard commented to the press that *Weser* could be worth as much as $1,500,000. She was renamed *Vancouver Island* and made a number of trips under that name and the Canadian flag until she was torpedoed by the U 558 on 15 October 1941 in the Atlantic with the loss of all on board. In July 1943 that submarine was caught in the Bay of Biscay by aircraft of the RAF and US Army Air Force. An American Liberator severely damaged the submarine, which was finished off by a Halifax aircraft of the RAF. The German commanding officer was Kapitanleutnant Krech who had commanded when *Vancouver Island* was sunk. He was one of five of his crew who were rescued by HMCS *Athabaskan*.

Prince Robert received numerous congratulatory messages. Prime Minister King, Angus L. Macdonald, Minister of National Defence for the Naval Service, and the Admiralty, all sent glowing words of congratulations. Commander Beard was later awarded a Mention in Dispatches. Lieutenant Commander Hope was given an OBE for the *Weser* and other later duties, while Petty Officer Moist was given a Mention in Dispatches for his service in AMCs. For a very new ship's company in a ship that had been rushed into service, they had indeed done well. They gave all Canada a lift

Officers of Prince Robert early 1942
Front Row – Kennedy, McDuff, Hope, Hart, Hinchcliffe, Accounts Officer, Senior (E)
Middle Row – NK, NK, Taylor, MacDonnell, NK, Rook, Dorcus NK
Back Row – Penhorn, NK, Jones, NK, NK, NK, NK, Levy
Some not identified – Elkins, Jennings, Saythers. Courtesy Penn Taylor

when other naval news was not very positive.

It is not surprising that naval leadership saw the possibility of future success of this nature since German merchant ships were still in various ports. Commander Beard left the ship, and the new Commanding Officer was Commander Frederick Hart RCN. He was a graduate of the 1913 term from the Royal Naval College of Canada and had served at sea with the Royal Navy in his early appointments. He assumed his new responsibilities on 8 October 1940, and the ship sailed two days later.

The following section is taken as a slightly modified quote from MacLeod's paper, which very colourfully describes the routine patrols so often experienced by naval ships in wartime, where life on board was a very high percentage of routine and a very low percentage of excitement. *Prince Robert* was ordered to watch for SS *Prahova*, a German-owned ship that had sailed from Talcahuano, Chile on 27 September. *Prince Robert* conducted a thorough search off the coast of Lower California, but without success. It later developed that *Prahova* had slipped into San Pedro, California on 23 October. *Prince Robert* then continued on to Puntarenas and to Callao, Peru. She paid calls at these ports, gathering information on the enemy merchant ships in harbour, estimating their condition and their likelihood of sailing. Leaving Callao on 28 October, she set course further south for Antofagasta, Chile, only to learn en route that the German merchantman *Osorno* was considered ready to sail from Talcahuano. Course was therefore altered north again, and she maintained a patrol off Talcahuano from 1 to 12 November. No breakout being detected, the new auxiliary cruiser entered the port to pay official calls and have a look-see as to what was happening. It was then found that *Osorno* was not at that time in a condition to sail.

In an attempt to fool the Germans, *Prince Robert* proceeded along the Chilean coast and called at Valparaiso, thence returning for a six-day patrol off Talcahuano from 18 to 24 November. There followed a leave period at Antofagasta and a call at Callao, Peru, to check enemy shipping. A rendezvous with the new 17,000 ton Royal fleet Auxiliary tanker *Bishopdale* was arranged for fueling but canceled when it was reported that the *Hermonthis* was planning to leave Callao on 2 December

A patrol off Callao was maintained until 14 December, when a visit to that port revealed that *Hermonthis* was not ready to sail. It was not until the 30 January 1941 that the monotony of the constant patrolling off the Chilean coast was broken again. While *Prince Robert* had been watching the approaches to Callao in December, the SS *Portland*, reported to be carrying some twenty fugitives from the *Graf Spee*, had sneaked down the coast from Coquimbo and into Talcahuano. After Christmas, the Canadian ship maintained a month-long patrol off the port, broken only by brief meetings with *Bishopdale* for refueling. Even this was good seamanship experience, as fueling at sea is no easy matter for the inexperienced.

Word was finally received in the early hours of 30 January that the *Portland* had sailed. *Prince Robert*, who was at that time about 50 miles northwest of Talcahuano, immediately commenced a curve search that would enable her to intercept the enemy merchantman. Soon this plan was abandoned, intelligence being received that *Portland* was bound for Puerto Montt, Chile, a small port in the Gulf of Ancud some 400 miles south of Valparaiso, the capital of Chile. Proceeding at full speed, *Prince Robert* arrived at the Canal Chacao early in the following morning and transited the Canal into the Gulf. The *Portland* was not in the Gulf and surmising that she had preceded the merchantman, the Canadian ship lay in wait at the entrance to the Canal.

While all this patrolling was taking place off the coast of South America, Ottawa had decided that *Prince Robert* could be employed in convoy duties of troop transports and refrigerator ships originating in New Zealand. *Prince Henry* would soon be ready to provide a relief for *Prince Robert* in looking for German blockade runners.

The New Zealand authorities were reacting to the possible presence of German raiders that had recently sunk ships in their area. So the elderly RN cruiser HMS *Diomede* relieved *Prince Robert* in early February. The principal concern was the presence of two German merchant raiders, the *Orion* and the *Komet*. Between them they had sunk 23 ships totaling over 100,00 tons during the period from April 1940 to November 1941. Both returned to Germany without meeting any opposition. *Komet* sailed on a second cruise in November 1942 but was torpedoed and sunk by the Royal Navy Motor Torpedo Boat *MTB 236* in the English Channel. *Orion* did other duties in home waters but was sunk by Russian aircraft in May of 1945.

In response to the New Zealand Naval Board, *Prince Robert* undertook one troop convoy run while Ottawa made plans for her future employment. The troops, mostly airmen, were destined for Canada to join the Commonwealth Air Training Plan. Arriving at Suva on 27 February 1941 *Prince Robert* took over escort from the New Zealand Armed Merchant Cruiser HMNZS *Monowai*. Her convoy consisted of the SS *Awatea*, a 13,000 ton liner. This would be the first of several long trans-Pacific passages when *Robert* escorted the elegant 22 knot *Awatea* bringing Australian and New Zealand airmen across the ocean for training. Both ships arrived in Esquimalt on 16 March after an uneventful voyage.

Prince Robert returned to Esquimalt for a refit period that lasted from mid March until mid April. In addition to minor repairs she received her much delayed Colt 0.5 anti-aircraft weapons and had "A" and "Y" six inch guns transposed to correct a training problem. She also had an extension to her bilge keels, which was intended to reduce her excessive rolling.

Prince Robert made one more escort run. But before it was begun she was diverted to Honolulu where she fueled. Intelligence had learned that four German airmen had sailed on the American liner *President Garfield*, whose destination was Japan. With the full knowledge of the American government *Prince Robert* intercepted the *President Garfield* and boarded her. The liner's captain made no objections to the boarding party and quickly provided identification of the Germans, who were then removed to *Prince Robert* as prisoners. Other German seamen stranded in the US did escape to Japan but in Japanese NYK ships. American authorities, still officially neutral, could not prevent them. They therefore agreed to Germans taking the *President* ships to Japan, but were not too reluctant to give over their passengers. In early May, *Prince Robert* met the cruiser HMNZS *Achilles* and relieved her of the escorted ship *Awatea*. The liner and *Prince Robert* arrived in Esquimalt in mid May.

Ottawa had now agreed that *Prince Robert* would continue with the escort of troop ships for the period to end in August of 1941. During that period her movements would be controlled by New Zealand naval authorities. *Prince Robert's* duties were to escort the ships from New Zealand to the central Pacific where they were deemed sufficiently safe to continue on their own to Esquimalt. The first convoy originated in Suva in late May with SS *Aorangi*. The second began in Auckland, in mid June with *Awatea,* and the third also began in Auckland with SS *Dominion Monarch* which carried some valuable cargo as well as 1,200 Royal Australian Air Force bound for training in Canada. That convoyed ship transited the Panama Canal and met *Prince David* for passage north in the Atlantic.

This type of duty for *Prince Robert* was somewhat dull for the ship's company but it was also a period where men new to the sea and to the navy could get their sea legs and be more fully trained in all the daily duties and action stations that are so important when more exciting events are experienced.

When *Prince Robert* was en route back to Auckland a modest flurry of excitement did occur. It was described in the MacLeod's paper as follows, "Course had been shaped for Auckland at a moderate speed, when orders arrived from the New Zealand Navy Board for *Prince Robert* to return with despatch. Intelligence reports indicated that a Japanese vessel tied up in Los Angeles was loading spare engine parts for a damaged German vessel in the Pacific. It was thought that the supply ship would rendezvous with the raider in a secluded cove at the Chilean Easter Island. *Prince Robert's* task was to find her and to then take appropriate action. She arrived at Auckland on 28 July, took on fuel, and sailed east the same day. Guns' crews were exercised vigorously on passage, while following weather pushed her along to her destination twenty-four hours ahead of schedule. Easter Island was sighted at 0600 7 August. The ship went to action stations, rang up full speed, closed and circumnavigated the small island. The coves and anchorages were thoroughly investigated, but no ship was seen.

Captain Hart, with his Navigator Lieutenant AR Dykes RCNR, Sub-Lieutenant (Special Branch) SA Dezall RCNVR, borne for intelligence duties, and an interpreter changed into plain clothes and went ashore to look around. They found no enemy, only the Island's new Governor Commandante Pasquale Reid, a Chilean of German descent, and the Catholic priest Father Sebastian Englert, a German alright but as he stressed, no Nazi. The last ship seen had been nine months earlier, the once-a-year visit of the single vessel that came regularly to the island. This intelligence was believed, and was indeed accurate; the Canadians found the folk ashore very friendly and respectful, though curious, and formed the opinion that they were essentially pro-British. They would probably have seemed friendly still, just as nosy, and pro-German had the disguised raider *Komet* arrived instead of *Prince Robert* to relieve their distant, tranquil monotony"

Thinking that the German ship had chosen another of the Pacific islands, *Prince Robert* looked into the small islands of Sala Y Gomez north of Easter Island. Finding nothing there, she refueled at the west coast Peruvian port of Talara on the western most point of South America and then sailed on 14 August for Auckland. While in Talara she suffered her first casualty when a sailor overdid his leave by excessive alcohol consumption. The local drink is "pisco", a drink that needs care. Soon after sailing *Prince Robert's* orders were changed. A message ordered her to make a north west course to return home to Esquimalt.

Naval intelligence was aware of the presence in the Pacific Ocean of the German raider *Komet*. A ship of just 3,287 tons, she carried six 15 cm guns as main armament, some mines, an Arado 196 A1 search aircraft and a crew of 194. She was not unlike the raider *Thor* which had defeated AMCs on more than one occasion. *Komet* had sailed from Germany in July 1940 and had reached the Pacific across the top of Russia by way of the Northeast Passage. Captain Eyssen of the *Komet* had planned the trip and Stalin had approved it after a large German payment had been made. Eyssen described the journey after the war. The Soviet icebreakers *Lenin* and *Stalin* had assisted the passage and the Russians persisted in the charade of apparently not knowing the true nature of the raider. From late 1940 until August of 1941 *Komet* had had limited success, sinking a few ships but was frequently alone in the broad sea. She was certainly in the general vicinity of *Prince Robert* in August of 1941 and the two ships might have met. *Komet* was south of the Galapagos Islands and sank the British ship *Astralind* on 14 August. But the possibly fateful meeting did not take place, although the two ships were later noted to have passed within 100 miles when *Prince Robert* crossed *Komet's* bows. *Robert* sailed north and *Komet* returned to Germany via Cape Horn and the Atlantic Ocean.

Malcolm Macleod's paper suggests that in a ship-to-ship engagement *Prince Robert* might have been sunk but would have damaged *Komet*. That ship would have been difficult to repair, and also would have announced her position for other naval units to find her. At least *Robert* would have fulfilled the function of an AMC "to fight such an action against superior materiel. All this would sharpen the focus of Allied naval dispositions and decreased the likelihood of further depredations from at least one enemy source." In retrospect this seems to be an excessive price to pay for a few items of naval intelligence that might or might not have been useful.

Prince Robert reached Esquimalt on 24 August 1941 and went into planned refit on 8 September.

MacLeod's paper provides the strategic background for the next phase in the life of *Prince Robert*. It is a tragic one and has resulted in many recriminations over the years since the war ended. The paper says that "Japan was continuing restless in the Far East, and Great Britain could not ignore the facts. She would be deeply involved if hostilities broke out in the Pacific, and such an eventuality would find her woefully unprepared to defend her widespread interest there, committed as she was to the death-struggle in Europe. But that same struggle necessitated the maintenance of all available troops at home, and it was recognized that the garrison at Hong Kong, which was the British outpost closest to the sources of Japanese aggression could provide only token resistance to a determined attack.

The token should be offered but beleaguered Britain could not afford any reinforcements to add to the Royal Scots and Middlesex Regiments already in Hong Kong. This was the hard-headed but common-sense view that prevailed at Downing Street through the first half of 1941. It was altered – unfortunately as the event proved in the summer by staff pressure to strengthen Hong Kong. The British Prime Minister yielded to the suggestion that Canada be approached to provide two battalions as reinforcements for the Hong Kong garrison."

The Canadian Government agreed to send one battalion each of the Royal Rifles of Canada from Quebec and of the Winnipeg Grenadiers, all designated as Force C. The battalions consisted of 96 officers and 1877 other ranks. Also in the group were two nursing

"C" Company of Royal Rifles of Canada on board Prince Robert November 1941 Library and Archives of Canada PR I 14820

sisters, two medical officers in addition to the regimental medical officers, two officers of the Canadian Dental Corps and their assistants, three Chaplains, some members of the Royal Canadian Corps of Signals and a detachment of the Canadian Postal Corps. Their mobile equipment was to follow but never did reach them.

Prince Robert took some of the officers and men but the majority was embarked in the *Awatea* in Vancouver. The New Zealand liner had been officially requisitioned as a troopship in 1941. While in Vancouver some work to reconfigure her as a transport had been carried out. *Awatea* would be bombed and sunk in November 1942 off Algeria during the Allied landings in North Africa.

The two ships arrived in Honolulu on 14 November 1941, where they were joined by HMS *Danae*, a light cruiser. The remainder of the journey to Hong Kong was without serious incident except for one course change to avoid possible Japanese naval forces. The troops were disembarked in late November. They had little time

Group of Royal Rifles of Canada after the fall of Hong Kong Library and Archives of Canada copy number PR 116579

to prepare. When the Japanese struck a hopeless but courageous fight ensued. Of the 1,974 who were landed, 556 died either in the fighting for Hong Kong or in prisoner camps. Those who were set free at war's end had suffered untold privations. Many returned to Canada with broken health and deep hatred for the treatment that they had received. *Prince Robert* played a role in the last act of the Hong Kong drama as will be seen later in this narrative.

Prince Robert's return journey was not without potential drama as well. She left Hong Kong on 19 November, spent a day in Honolulu, and set course for Esquimalt on 22 November. Post-war lore has developed a suggestion that a flare sighted on the night of 6 December might have in some way been identified as coming from the Japanese fleet that was en route to the position from which

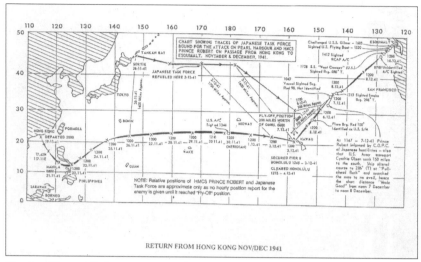

RETURN FROM HONG KONG NOV/DEC 1941

Track of Prince Robert on return from Hong Kong Courtesy of Bill Johnson

it attacked Pearl Harbour. The tracks of both parties have been closely examined and show without any possible other conclusion that they were never closer that 500 miles from each other. But interviews with *Prince Robert* veterans as late as 2002 will find the story being told that they missed the Japanese fleet by very little. Bill Johnson included a track chart in his 1988 booklet which we include and are pleased to acknowledge its source. It shows the positions and times of the various participants and makes it clear that *Prince Robert* could not have given warning of the Japanese fleet.

Prince Robert did receive a message advising her that Canada was at war with Japan. She was ordered to close the position of a US Army troop transport that had been torpedoed. On arrival at the area a search found nothing in spite of a clear night and full moon. Post war records have shown that the ship *Cynthia Olson* had been sunk with the loss of 33 crew members and two US Army personnel. The ship had been en route from Tacoma to Honolulu.. She had been a steam schooner of just over 2,000 tons.

Three Princes Armed

The Japanese submarine that had fired the torpedo was *I 26*, a particularly effective unit of the Japanese fleet. Later in the war she put a torpedo into the USS *Saratoga* and sank the American light cruiser USS *Juneau* . The *I 26* was destroyed in the Western Pacific on 18 November 1944 by the destroyer USS *Lawrence C. Taylor* and aircraft from the USS *Anzio*. *Prince Robert* arrived in Esquimalt on 10 December 1941.

H.M.C.S. Prince Henry

Prince Henry was the last of the three to begin conversion to an Armed Merchant Cruiser, and required much work to bring her to a satisfactory condition. Before all the work was completed at Vickers in Montreal she was taken over from the contractor and was steamed for Halifax with the assistance of an icebreaker to avoid being iced in for several more months. So it was not until the 4th of December 1940 that she commissioned under Captain Ron Agnew RCN, a 1911 graduate of the Royal Naval College of Canada who was to finish his naval career as a Commodore. More work took place in Halifax, and by the middle of January

Prince Henry in the St. Lawrence shortly after commissioning Courtesy
Commander Alf Wurtele

1941 some defects were corrected, stores were on board and the armaments, similar 6-inch guns to *Prince Robert,* and also from the British supply for AMCs stored in Canada, had been installed.

Prince Henry sailed for Bermuda to conduct her work-ups. For weeks the ship's company exercised at the guns and boat work in recognition of the expected role she would be required to fulfill. The gunners experienced the usual problem of laying and training the six-inch guns when the ship was rolling. Retired Captain Vern Howland was a Paymaster Lieutenant on the bridge and recalls her first main armament shoot. The salvo sprayed the tug towing the target and *Prince Henry* received an urgent light signal "Fire at the target not the tug." The Executive officer was Acting Commander RCN Alf Wurtele. He remembers two of his sailors who overstayed their leave in Hamilton, Bermuda. To return to their ship the next morning they talked the Royal Navy's Admiral Barge coxswain into stowing them in the fore-peak. Half way to Ireland Island the fore hatch sprang open and two green sailors were violently ill on the Admiral's sparkling barge. The *Henry* was not popular.

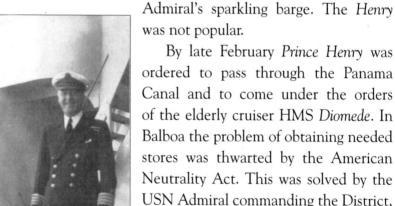

By late February *Prince Henry* was ordered to pass through the Panama Canal and to come under the orders of the elderly cruiser HMS *Diomede.* In Balboa the problem of obtaining needed stores was thwarted by the American Neutrality Act. This was solved by the USN Admiral commanding the District, who declared that the stores were

Prince Henry's commanding officer Captain R.I. Agnew Courtesy Ernest Smedley

Three Princes Armed

required under Lend Lease, an act not invoked until two weeks later.

Prince Henry met up with HMS *Diomede* on 1 March. Royal Navy intelligence had determined that four German merchant ships were expected to try to break out of the port of Callao, Peru as soon as conditions were right. After a period of patrolling the coasts of Peru and Costa Rica, *Prince Henry* entered the harbour of Callao on 24 March. She anchored just two cables from the German ships, where it was determined that the Germans were fueled and were ready to sail. Agnew was aware that the merchant ships had a speed of eleven knots and were most likely fitted with demolition (scuttling) charges to prevent capture. The belief was that more than one would sail, and they would take different courses once at sea. Japan was the likely direction they would choose. The four Germans were *Hermonthis, Muenchen, Monserrate* and *Leipzig*. These ships were all fairly recently built and were of 5,000 tons.

Prince Henry resumed her patrol off the port of Callao. Captain Agnew brought his ship near the harbour exit each evening, and during daylight hours moved further out to sea. He did this for ten days. Finally a signal reached him that the Germans had requested authority and had sailed at 1930 on the evening of the 31st March. Careful to avoid Peruvian waters, Agnew patrolled on a wide search area. His courses were based on an assumed enemy speed and direction. According to Commander Wurtele, Agnew had directed his officers into study groups to suggest the possible plan of escape by the German ships. Most of the groups assumed a run for Japan. With his ship's company at action stations and after eight hours of search *Muenchen* was sighted at a distance of 15 miles. The German altered course to the north. After a pursuit of less than an hour, *Henry* drew in to 12,000 yards and signaled "Stop instantly or I will open fire." The German kept her course so at 0700 Agnew fired one round which crossed the freighter's bows. The German slowed at once, but smoke and flames were

German ship Muenchen on fire 1 April 1941 Courtesy Commander Alf Wurtele

seen issuing from the after end of her superstructure. The shot, and the appearance of flames, so nearly coincided that the Captain was heard to sourly remark to the officer of "A" gun, "Now look what you've done!" Wurtele stated that the demolition of *Muenchen* was well organized by the Germans, as was their abandoning ship into life boats along with their German shepherd, Pietza.

The Germans began to man their boats, leaving *Muenchen* in a cloud of black smoke. Ordinary Seaman Norm Anderson was a bridge lookout when Captain Agnew noticed a German attempting to remove the tarpaulins from one of the hatches to fan the flames with fresh air. Agnew ordered Anderson to fire a few rounds from the bridge Sten gun, which caused the German to move away from the hatch. As Agnew drew near he could see that the ship was well alight and the flames were too fierce to allow her to be salvaged.

Three Princes Armed

Prince Henry's boarding party. Seaman Norm Anderson 4th from left
Courtesy Ernest Smedley

*Captain Agnew at Action
Stations in pajama pants* Courtesy
Ernest Smedley

Henrietta, Prince Henry's cat, in six inch gun barrel Courtesy Ernest Smedley

With the *Hermonthis* also at sea, *Prince Henry* altered course to the south and went to full speed. When that German freighter was found hours later it too was on fire, and by the time *Prince Henry* approached the crew had abandoned ship. Agnew sent away a boarding party in a cutter which picked up some of the Germans to take them back on board to help fight the fires and flooding. The salvage party shut the sea cocks. But after four hours of fighting the fire with limited equipment (hoses had been run across from *Henry* but they had no portable pump) and the two ships pounding against each other, it was decided that the ship could not be saved, and the men were withdrawn. After picking up more of the Germans from their life boats, *Prince Henry* sank *Hermonthis* with 33 rounds of gunfire. When she went to find what had eventually happened to *Muenchen* she learned that the Peruvian cruiser *Almirante Grau* had already sunk the German as a "danger to navigation."

Prince Henry was ordered to resume her patrol duties with attention to the Callao and Antofagasta areas. No German ship

Three Princes Armed

German prisoners on board Prince Henry Courtesy Ernest Smedley

sailed during this period, and *Henry* was recalled to Esquimalt on 29 April, arriving in that Canadian port on 9 May 1941. Her ship's company were now much more ready to face the next challenge that the developing war at sea had to offer them. Captain Agnew was later awarded a Mention in Dispatches for stopping the two German merchant ships from escaping.

Prince Henry's refit was a cursory one and limited to necessary repairs plus shielding for her high angle guns. She came out of Dockyard hands on 23 July 1941, and sailed locally to give her new members some experience. At that time in the war Canada was building corvettes and minesweepers rapidly, and sailors with a little sea experience were being drafted to the new ships to provide them with even a modicum of trained men. This was a problem for the RCN throughout the war. The navy grew from a pre-war total of 397 officers and 2276 ratings as charted in Gilbert Tucker's *Naval Service of Canada*. Of those the non-regulars were 206 officers and 477 men, either RCNR or RCNVR. Over 100,000 served by the end of the war but rarely did a ship return to either Halifax or Esquimalt without a number of her experienced personnel being drafted to new construction, and replaced by new faces.

Prince Henry sailed as *Prince Robert* was arriving back to Esquimalt. *Henry*'s mission was to seek out the raider (*Komet*) which had sunk ships near the Galapagos Islands. On arrival in that area on 31 August she was directed to meet HMS *Despatch,* a light cruiser, and the two ships set up a search pattern. *Prince Henry* encountered two ships, both of which were friendly. In the second incident the British steamer *Surrey* thought she was being chased by a German raider and broadcast a "raider in sight" message, an echo of *Robert*'s experience. *Henry* closed to within four miles of the *Surrey*. That ship then properly used the correct procedure of challenge and reply. In closing *Surrey, Prince Henry* might have suffered grievously had the ship been a raider.

Komet was not found so by 8 September *Prince Henry* broke off the hunt and transited the Panama Canal, arriving in Bermuda on the 25th. Her first duty was as escort to Halifax of the troop ship *Capetown Castle.* In October she patrolled with another AMC, HMS *Circassia,* later like *Henry* herself converted to a troop landing ship and landing Canadians at Sicily in mid-1943. The object was to find German raiders or support ships. None were discovered, and by early November *Prince Henry* was in Halifax where she was fitted out with Radio Direction Finding equipment (RDF, officially known after 1943 by the American term radar). She rounded out the year in a somewhat inglorious role as depot ship (barracks accommodation) for sailors in St. Johns, Newfoundland, while proper buildings were being constructed.

It was during this period that a change of command took place. Captain J.C.I. Edwards RCN, the new Commanding Officer, had been in the second term at the Royal Naval College of Canada. As did his contemporaries he had served much of his time in ships of the Royal Navy. He was an accomplished athlete and known by all as "Dutchy" for some undisclosed reason.

The outbreak of war with Japan meant that there was a need for more ships for patrol, and *Prince Henry* was brought from her role as a depot ship and back into action as an AMC. Her personnel were brought up to strength. She was now placed under the operational control of the US Navy and on arrival in San Juan, Puerto Rico, in mid January took her orders from the Commander Caribbean Sea Frontier. He was only able to provide the ship with aircraft maps, without any depths thereon, which was the cause of some anxiety on occasion when approaching unfamiliar shorelines. In San Juan, Howland also remembers Henry's sailors taking on too much of the cheap rum. So *Prince Henry* was banished to the quieter port of Charlotte Amalie.

Patrol duties began again. This time she spent the period until late February in the area of the Virgin and Leeward Islands with occasional refueling stops in St. Thomas. The monotony of patrol was broken when *Prince Henry* received orders to close the American ship SS *Lihue* which had been torpedoed on the 23rd by KL Albrecht Achilles in *U 161*. Rohwer in his book Axis Submarine Successes, reports that the *Lihue* "fought back after the first hit and dodged one torpedo." By the time *Prince Henry* arrived on the scene there was a tanker present that was rescuing the crew of *Lihue*.

There was also an aircraft overhead that dropped bombs forward of the stricken ship. Assuming the presence of a submarine, Captain Edwards decided to draw off to consider the possibility of saving the ship. A volunteer party was put on board and got the *Lihue* slowly underway. The party, under Commander Ron Jackson had to jettison the forward deck cargo and also try to get steam up. It required collecting enough wood in lieu of coal to get pressure in the boilers to get feed pumps working. They got the ship underway. The next day the weather deteriorated and *Lihue* was taken in tow by the USS *Partridge*, a minesweeper. *Prince Henry* sailed to

Crew of Delvalle rescued by Prince Henry April 1942 Author's collection

St. Lucia where she later learned that, despite all their combined efforts, *Lihue* had sunk on the 26th.

Prince Henry performed one more very useful duty before her time in the Caribbean came to a close. On 12th April she was informed that the British merchant ship *Delvalle* had been torpedoed (by *U 154* KK Walther Kolle*). Proceeding to the coordinates given, Edwards took a Catalina aircraft under his orders. Rafts were soon found and 44 survivors, including three women, were taken on board. One of the survivors said two lifeboats had also taken some of the crew. One of these was found by the aircraft, and *Prince Henry* took forty-four survivors to Jamaica. The other boat was not found.

By the middle of April the need for ships on Canada's West Coast overshadowed the value of an AMC in the Caribbean. Canada obtained the release of *Prince Henry* from American control and she sailed for Esquimalt where she arrived on 7 May 1942. She joined her two sister ships, the first time all three *Princes* were to operate together.

H.M.C.S. Prince David

The RCN started the war with a very limited number of uniformed personnel. There were sufficient to man the six destroyers and a few minesweepers that constituted the fleet and modest shore establishment required for support. There was also the RCNVR in the 18 cities where a Reserve unit had been established, and many of these men were soon at one of the coasts being trained or drafted to a ship. The third component of the naval establishment was the RCNR composed of men whose profession was the sea. On the West Coast was a separate entity referred to as "The Fishermen's Reserve." Many of the RCNR were professionals who had sailed in liners, merchant ships and other deep-sea craft. Similar to the system in the Royal Navy, they were qualified Merchant Seamen officers who were granted commissions. *Prince David* commissioned on 19 December 1940 under Commander W.B. Armit RCNR. He had been standing by the ship since February of that year while it was undergoing conversion.

Officers of Prince David early 1942
Front Row 4th from left Rivers, 5th Morland, 6th Armit, 7th Shedden,
8th Arnison, 9th Koughan. Others not identified in the picture, King, Ross
Carter, Thomas, Lloyd and Sullivan.
Geoff Shedden collection courtesy Naval and Military Museum, Calgary

With Naval Headquarters attempting to rush every available unit to sea it is a wonder that a ship's company could have been found and made available in the appropriate numbers and trades. Discussions with veterans of the three *Prince* ships many years later indicated that the men came from a wide variety of sources. Some recalled that many of the men, in particular the engine room personnel, had sailed in the *Princes* when they were operating as liners. One veteran said that he recalled shipmates who had been early deserters from Royal Navy ships during their visits to west coast ports. But the rest of the men were new, inadequately or poorly trained and unaccustomed to the class of ship to which they had been assigned.

Veterans frequently remember the lighter side of their service in ships. Commander W.G. "Geoff" Shedden recalls the first time that *Prince David* experienced very rough seas. The Principal Medical Officer's cabin was too far from the Sick Bay so he had moved and the Roman Catholic Padre got his old cabin. But the PMO plaque over the Padre's cabin door was not changed in the rush to get the ship ready. In the rough seas a Lieutenant was so sick he took to his bunk and asked a sailor to get the Doctor for him. The sailor found the PMO labeled cabin, woke the occupant (the Padre) and said the Lieutenant thought he was dying. The Padre put on his full vestments and appeared at the afflicted officer's door in order to give Last Rites. The officer, not an RC, had not realized that he was "in extremis."

Prince David's period of working-up off Bermuda was not completed when she was ordered to convoy protection for BHX 109 en route Bermuda to Halifax. She sailed from Bermuda on 11 February 1941. With no submarines as yet operating in those waters her role was to deter or fight German warships or commerce raiders. On returning to Bermuda on 16 February she grounded in the dredged channel. In her civilian period as a liner she had also grounded in the same area of Bermuda and had spent 36 hours in that condition before being floated free.

Prince David was floated off the following morning and sailed on 3 March with convoy BHX 113. On 8 March she was directed to find a possible German raider thought to be the armed merchantman Thor. That relatively small ship (3,144 tons) had been at sea since July, had sunk 12 ships totaling 53,000 tons, captured hundreds of prisoners and damaged two large British AMCs (HMS Alcantara and HMS Carnarvon Castle) with her six 5.9 inch guns. Prince David did not sight the raider and when she made port in Port of Spain, Trinidad, she passed HMS Voltaire, a 13,000 ton British AMC that was sailing. Voltaire, twice Price David's size, did meet the Thor and in a two hour engagement was sunk. Thor had greater gun range and her gunners were obviously highly trained and accurate. Of the crew of Voltaire, 197 were taken prisoner. Had Prince David met Thor it is likely she would have suffered the same fate.

In the spring of 1941 Prince David was steaming alone when Captain Armit on the bridge asked his Executive Officer, Geoff Shedden to observe what appeared to be the upper works of a major warship. When asked his opinion as to what action Armit should take, Shedden, said he was going aft to his action station because the first target the enemy would aim at was the bridge. Later intelligence suggested that the warship may have been a German pocket battleship. Able Seaman Neil Tomlinson wrote to author McKee in 1984 that that ship's company had no illusions about what the ship could do in action. Even the Padre was heard to say, "If we ever get into action I'm going to the stern and jump in."

Prince David spent the latter part of March in Bermuda. Commander Armit was ill and Commander Ken Adams RCN was brought from Halifax to take command on 25 March. Ken Adams was a 1919 Royal Naval College of Canada graduate who had left the RCN for merchant service. He returned to the regular navy in 1928 and had numerous sea appointments.

Prince David's next duty on 5 April was to search for possible evidence of HMS *Voltaire*. She did find a large oil patch and some debris that merely showed that a large ship had been sunk. She was then ordered to set up a patrol area east and north of the French Caribbean Island of Martinique. The Vichy government of conquered France was no longer trusted by Great Britain. It was for that reason and to prevent the existing French fleet from being taken over by Germany that the highly controversial attack of the French fleet at Dakar had taken place, an action causing the utmost bitterness by French citizenry. This Royal Navy action was to cause a lasting enmity between France and Britain throughout the war. Any French naval or merchant ships still at sea or in foreign ports was the object of British naval intelligence to determine their intentions and possible sailing dates. Some French merchant ships were in United States ports and the Americans were making it difficult for them to clear the required documentation. One of these was the 13,500 ton *Sheharazade* in New Orleans. When that ship sailed without gaining approval *Prince David* was in Bermuda. She sailed on 21st April but the R.N. cruiser HMS *Diomede* took over the capture, and *David* returned to Bermuda.

The remainder of *Prince David*'s time on the east coast consisted of uneventful patrols. She took the Commander-in-Chief America and West Indies to Halifax in June, escorted convoy BHX 135 also in June, did some more patrolling in July, another convoy, BHX 137 in July and in August escorted a troopship to Halifax. Later in August while on patrol with the British AMC HMS *Circasia*, *David* sighted and chased an unidentified ship, which she thought might be a cruiser. She was unable to gain on the departing ship. Later information suggested that it was the German supply ship *Python*. (*Python* scuttled herself when intercepted by HMS *Dorsetshire* in December 1941.)

In late August *Prince David* was again on patrol when she found the British merchant ship *St. Margaret* with serious engine trouble and unable to proceed. Ken Adams decided to take her under tow and brought her into Bermuda on 3 September. Under maritime law salvage payment was awarded to the ship's company of *Prince David*. After years of legal wrangling and problems in finding eligible recipients an amount of about $3,500 was divided up among them. (This was according to Malcolm Macleod in the 1965 DHist. paper). The authors have a copy of a letter from the Naval Secretary to Commander Roderick C. Carter and dated 5 July 1948. The letter enclosed his cheque for $32.61. It was his share of Salvage Money for salvage of SS *St. Margaret*. The shares ranged from 60 for the Captain down to three shares for an Ordinary Seaman.

Salvage money is distinct from Prize Money. Numerous sources said that the prize money coming to all navies of the Commonwealth as a result of the capture of enemy ships was pooled and distributed to the officers and men at the end of the war. In fact the Canadian share of the total was not given to the sailors but was donated to the Naval Benevolent Fund. (To author F.M. McKee's annoyance, who would like to have received sailing era Prize Money).

Later in September *Prince David* was directed to join the escort for the British liner *Durban Castle*. That ship had on board King George II of the Hellenes and senior members of the Greek government who were being evacuated to the United Kingdom. On 15th September David relieved the cruiser HMS *Newcastle* and joined the AMC HMS *Queen of Bermuda* as the small group headed for England. Very soon they were met by a severe gale which did not permit *David* to maintain the required speed and course alterations due to her ship's violent movements. *David* detached from the convoy but Adams was later awarded the Greek War Cross Third Class for *David*'s part in the escort. *Prince David* arrived in Halifax on 20th September for a planned period of maintenance.

A change of command for *Prince David* took place in December. The new captain was Valentine Godfrey RCN. He was a 1913 Royal Naval College of Canada graduate who had spent much of

CANADA

Department of National Defence

Naval Service

5 JUL 1948 .... 194......

OUR FILE .... NS. 3852-412/1 NS,
NA. (P-3), 0-12670 .

YOUR FILE ....

REGISTERED

Dear Sir:

      Enclosed herewith is Official Cheque No.
B/4-06/256 for $ 32.61 representing
20 shares of the Salvage Money awarded to the
Ship's Company of H.M.C.S. "PRINCE DAVID" for salvage
services rendered to S.S. "ST. MARGARET" during the
period 28th August, 1941, to 3rd September, 1941.

      For your information the total distribution
of Salvage Money amounted to $3423.37 divided in 2099
shares on the following basis:

Commander in Command	— 60	shares
Commander not in Command	— 30	"
Lieutenant Commander not in Command	— 25	"
→Lieutenant not in Command	— 20	"
Sub-Lieutenant not in Command	— 15	"
Commissioned Officer not in Command	— 15	"
Warrant Officer not in Command	— 12	"
Chief Petty Officer	— 10	"
Petty Officer	— 8	"
Leading Rating	— 6	"
Able Rating	— 5	"
Ordinary Rating	— 3	"

Yours truly,

Encl.

NAVAL SECRETARY.

Cdr. Roderick C. Carter, RCN(R) (Retired),
4157 Cavendish Ave.,
Apt. 25,
MONTREAL, P.Q.

D 2258
1000M—7-43 (1188)
N.S. #15-5-2258

Letter awarding salvage money Author's collection

his career with the Royal Navy that included time in submarines.
He ended his career after the war as a Commodore.

    Commander Godfrey took his ship to sea almost immediately
and brought her into Esquimalt on 30 December 1941. His refit in
Halifax had barely been completed, and many of the ship's more
experienced personnel had been drafted off. She was then sent to
the West Coast and the long passage west was a period of training

the new men. The negative aspects of long days on patrol for all three of the Prince ships was partly mitigated by the fact that it was a time to indoctrinate many of those who were new to the navy and to the sea. These men took their experience and skills to the corvettes, minesweepers and frigates that were joining the fleet in increasingly large numbers.

The Three Princes On The West Coast 1942-1943

The entry of Japan into the war changed some of the disposition of Canadian naval ships. The West Coast was now seen as a possible area of action. At the time of the Pearl Harbour attack the officer commanding in Esquimalt had a very limited number of assets. Other than *Prince Robert* that in December was returning to port, there were just three corvettes, some minesweepers, a couple of armed yachts and a collection of smaller craft of the "Fishermen's Reserve." Added to the Japanese threat was the fact that by late 1941 and early 1942 the course of the war at sea was more evident to the planners in Ottawa and it was not going well. German surface raiders after the *Bismarck* episode in May 1941 were less of concern of convoys to Great Britain. Now the U-boat was the threat and anti-submarine vessels were needed in great numbers. The *Prince* ships did not fit into the scenes of action on the East Coast. And the civilian population was becoming nervous about the ever expanding Japanese threat.

For Commodore W.J.R. Beech, RCN who in December was commanding in Esquimalt, his needs were vessels that could patrol the long coast line and its myriad bays and inlets. Lieutenant Bill Johnson noted that the ships' duties were to patrol focal shipping points, patrol sheltered waters, be a presence, and make credible publicized threats against the enemy. Added to these were the strategic purposes of countering American pressure of taking responsibility in Canadian waters, and secondly, to make the Japanese believe that any attacks could be firmly met.

To acknowledge these factors both *Prince Henry* and *Prince David* were brought around to Esquimalt. *Robert* and *David* commenced a series of patrol schedules in early 1942. *Prince Henry* joined them later in the year. It was a period of constant adjustment to find the most effective way of keeping the maximum amount of days at sea and still meet the ships' needs for maintenance and training. Sea conditions off Vancouver Island can become very rough at times, and there were not too many aids to navigation or pilotage except some lighthouses. The ships made the transit to patrol stations via the Straits of Juan de Fuca under orders to do so at night with navigation lights off. To Captain Frank Houghton of *Prince David* this was the greatest danger of the operation.

Perhaps one of Japan's greatest mistakes of the war was its use of submarines. Rather than execute an aggressive policy of attack on surface units of the merchant and naval fleets which would have required a major response tying up many vessels, Japan had deliberately adopted a policy of using its submarines in the reconnaissance role for its battle fleet. *I 26* had sunk the *Cynthia Olson* in December of 1941 but there must have been numerous targets exiting the Straits of Juan da Fuca.

The spring of 1942 was a period of patrol for the three *Prince* ships. This certainly was good training for the ships companies, but it is difficult in retrospect to decide what threat was felt to be most serious. If it was attack by an aircraft carrier there is nothing that an AMC could do. Major surface warships would not have operated that far from Japan, some 5,000 miles or nine days of steaming. That left submarines. Any battle between a submarine and an AMC would be heavily biased in favor of the submarine. But they chose to play a passive role. In preparation for the Japanese attack on the Aleutian Islands, two submarines had been sent to patrol in the area of the US/Canada international border. The official history of the Canadian Navy, "No Higher Purpose", states that there was some indication that *I 26* actually sighted one or more of the

Prince ships while on passage to its operational area. It chose not to attack.

Commander Tagami in *I 25* on 7 June 1942 had sunk the *Coast Trader* a US Army transport of 3,286 tons off Cape Flattery. On 20 June he put a torpedo into the Victoria built 7,126 ton *Fort Camosun*. With a cargo of B.C. lumber that ship remained afloat. The final acts of the two Japanese submarines before they returned home received much publicity in Canada but did little damage. Commander Minoru Yokata in *I 26* shelled the light house at Estevan Point on the west coast of Vancouver Island, north of Tofino, missing the building. Much air and naval activity followed this action, and it may have been Yokata's purpose to simply alarm the populace. He did that but he also gave all the auxiliary units a sense of purpose. It certainly alarmed the locals at least.

Commander Shedden training a boarding party on board Prince David Courtesy Naval and Military Museum, Calgary

Sunday Divisions on board Prince David Courtesy Naval and Military Museum, Calgary

The Aleutians Campaign
August – November 1942

In May of 1942 the Battle of Midway dominated the headlines, and in most naval histories it remains one of the most important events of the war. The force that sailed to occupy Midway Island was under the command of Admiral Chuichi Nagumo. In overall command was Admiral Isoroku Yamamoto. His command also contained two light aircraft carriers and other ships and transports whose purpose was to occupy the Aleutian Islands. Although the Japanese fleet suffered a devastating defeat at Midway they did achieve the occupation of the outer Aleutian islands of Attu and Kiska in early June.

Captain Roskill states in his War At Sea Volume II that when the Japanese took the islands in June of 1942 it was not to create a base for striking at Alaska or any other place on the mainland.

They wanted to deny the Americans the use of the Aleutian chain as stepping-stones to northern Japan. There is no evidence that the Americans had ever formulated a plan of that nature. The potential northern conditions and distances in the northern Pacific made such a combined operation much too risky. In a much larger strategic ploy the invasion was also intended to create a diversion so that the US Navy would send some of their fleet north while Midway was struck.

By the summer of 1942 the three Prince ships had been into refit where new equipment was fitted. *Prince Robert* and *Price David* received depth-charge throwers and asdic sets. These were also fitted to *Prince Henry,* as were two Oerliken anti-aircraft weapons. In July *David* was used to film the movie *Commandos Strike At Dawn,* a welcome diversion for the sailors. The Saanich Inlet and the West Coast represented occupied Norway for many scenes. The movie was directed by John Farrow, who had also directed the film *Corvette K225* and later was made an Honourary Commander in the RCNVR. Paul Muni was the leading man, with actresses Anna Lee and Lillian Gish as the female leads. The story was written by C.S. Forester of Hornblower fame. With many of the Canadian sailors interacting with the stars it provided memorable moments for letters home. Val Godfrey had a supporting role, playing the captain of his own ship.

The seizure of the Aleutians by the Japanese was as much an emotional blow to the Americans as it was a strategic loss. Theodore Roscoe in "United States Destroyer Operations" noted General Billy Bishop's statement "If Japan takes Alaska she can take New York." So the Americans had done some construction of naval and air bases at Dutch Harbour and Kodiak. Some patrols had been instituted, particularly by older US submarines of the "S" class. The waters were some of the most difficult and dangerous possible. The charts were in many cases inadequate, there were fogs, and the seas could suddenly rise.

Prince David in *"Commandos Strike At Dawn"* Courtesy Naval and Military Museum, Esquimalt, B.C.

When the Japanese struck the US commander had five cruisers, eleven destroyers and six submarines. By the time the Canadians entered the operations there had been some serious naval actions. The Japanese had lost some destroyers to American submarines, and a submarine to a destroyer.

In June of 1942 Commanding Officer Pacific Coast (COPC) was asked by the Americans if the RCN could assist in operations in the Aleutian theater. Canada did not give a definitive reply until August, when COPC received a signal from Commander North West Sea Frontier that asked how many ships could be assigned. It further asked, in some renewed urgency that those ships report to Kodiak by 20 August. COPC took it upon himself to send the three *Prince* ships and the corvettes *Vancouver* and *Dawson*. NSHQ later concurred in that decision. The Americans would have preferred to have had more dedicated anti-submarine units. The decision to respond by COPC was not viewed lightly in Ottawa where the unsuitability of the *Prince* ships was not in doubt. But it was too late to rescind.

With today's sonar (asdic) equipment so sophisticated it is difficult to understand why an AMC with rudimentary capability to acquire, let alone prosecute, a submarine contact would be assigned to convoy duties. But that was the only role that the Americans decided that the *Princes* could fill. The sole benefit to the Americans was that at least some of their destroyers would be released for fleet duties. All five of the Canadian contribution arrived in Kodiak harbour on 20th August, with the corvettes berthing first. Captain Edwards asked the harbour authorities for berthing instructions. He was not happy when the reply came "Berth with the other corvettes" indicating the USN's lack of familiarity with their new Allies on the scene. The *Prince* ships almost immediately began escort duties.

The occupied islands of Attu and Kiska are at the end of the long chain that extends westward from the mainland. Joseph Schull used just two paragraphs to cover the Canadian participation in the Aleutians. He did emphasize the constant threat of an overwhelming Japanese naval force in the area with numerous submarines as

Captain Frank Houghton of Prince Robert 1942 Courtesy F.W. Bryan of Winnipeg

well as cruisers and destroyers. To the men in the Canadian ships it was the weather that dominated their lives. The fog, the wind (williwas), the seas, the lack of detailed charts and numerous hazards combined with the drudgery of steaming back and forth for the 600 mile convoy runs between Kodiak and Dutch Harbour made each day one of survival. For those on the bridge avoiding grounding and keeping clear of convoyed ships without reliable radar placed a heavy premium on their skills and that of their lookouts. Those who later went to duty in the harsh North Atlantic were never in doubt as to which area was the most severe.

The Canadians were designated "Force D" although the two corvettes rarely worked with the AMCs. The American plan was to isolate the Japanese occupied islands and to limit or deny them the chance of using the islands for further encroachment eastward.

As the three *Prince* ships settled in to two months of regular convoy runs there were no engagements with Japanese ships or aircraft. There were some incidents. In one convoy the merchant ship *Sartoria* grounded, and the *Prince Henry* stood by until a high tide released it after an attempt to tow it off was not successful. *Prince David* struck something that damaged a propeller. Both *Prince Henry* and *Prince David* believed that they had a submarine contact and dropped depth charges. And in one semi-comic occasion when in heavy fog an escorted ship astern of *Prince David* fired on *David's* streamed fog buoy believing it to be a submarine periscope. Captain Frank Houghton recalled this event in his article in "Salty Dips." He said that the fog buoy was in the shape of a barrel and was towed about 400 yards astern so that the next ship in line, unable to see the ship ahead, could at least follow the buoy. The merchant ship *Elias Howe* saw the buoy, sounded her emergency whistle, sheered off to port and fired a stream of machine-gun bullets. Later the Captain of *David* commended the ship on her "fine degree of alertness." It may have been privately a touch of sarcasm.

Prince Robert being addressed by a US Admiral, Aleutians. Author's collection

Captain Houghton also made note of his first convoy that consisted of about six merchant ships. As they were moving east they suddenly saw on radar that several ships indicated by blips were approaching. Aware of the Japanese cruisers he flashed the recognition signal. After the third signal with no response his gunners were prepared to fire. At that moment they were able to recognize an American destroyer escorting another group. Houghton was angry that he had not been advised of the American convoy in his area. After bringing his complaint to the USN Admiral he felt that matters improved and the two allies got along very well for the duration of the time that the Canadians served in that area. The ships survived the arduous route, the difficult weather and the presence of superior Japanese ships. According to Captain Edwards the most dangerous moment was when an American Army officer demonstrated his automatic rifle in the wardroom. He let off a blast "scattering the afternoon tea drinkers and irretrievably damaging pots in the galley above." Charles Dillon confirmed that incident and said that on another occasion a bullet from a .5 inch machine gun struck the galley when the weapon was being serviced. Vern Howland also recalled the bullets smashing into galley pots and how it frightened the cat Henrietta just as she was sipping her usual mid-afternoon brandy and condensed milk. Henrietta had been born on board and had never been ashore until the ship arrived in Kodiak. One experience with her pads on cold gravel and she never went ashore again.

The Accounts Officer on board *Prince Henry* was Lieutenant-Commander Charles Dillon. He had joined the RCNVR in 1931 as a Paymaster Cadet after receiving an earlier rejection letter for service as a Naval Cadet. In 1962 he received another letter advising him of his promotion to Rear Admiral. When interviewed he recalled that his ship never sighted any Japanese ships but were often reported by the RCAF patrol aircraft as Japanese warships. This would result in a "flash" message to all three *Prince* ships, who would then dash about trying to find each other. He also remembered that on their convoy route was a prominent undersea peak. This would be reported to the bridge as a submarine contact and thoroughly depth-charged each time. One sad side event took place on 16 July 1942 when six Kittyhawk fighters of RCAF 111 Squadron flew into a fog shrouded cliff. They were moving from their base in Anchorage to another base in the Aleutians.

For the Canadians the northern operations came to an end on 30th October. All three *Prince* ships departed for the south, *Prince Robert* as escort to two American ships and the other two AMCs in company with the two corvettes. They were all back in their home base of Esquimalt by 4th November.

The Aleutian campaign was not a significant part of Canada's naval history. The enemy was never met. But it meant a lot to those who were there. Many years after the war had ended, retired

Officers of Prince Henry mid 1942. Front row – Earnshaw, Baker, Stapley, Couvee. 2nd row – Denyer, Dillon, Young, Finch-Noyes, Edwards, Maheu, McMurtry. Back row – Gage, Cook, Horn, Ross, Base, Robitaille, Ridge, Brinkman, Howland, Dixon. Courtesy Rear Admiral Charles Dillon

Rear Admiral Charles Dillon was able to spearhead a successful attempt to have "the Aleutians" approved as a Battle Honour for the five Canadian participants.

The three *Prince* ships all returned to their accustomed role of patrol operating out of Esquimalt. For *Prince Robert* that ceased on 24th December when the ship went in for a major refit for a new role. The other two carried on until early March 1943. Captain Houghton of *Prince Robert* left that ship as she was paid off and went to command *Prince Henry* until 18th March 1943.

CHAPTER FOUR
1943 – 1945

Prince Robert

A New Role – A New Life – A New Captain

Tempora mutantur, et nos mutamur in illis.
William Harrison 1577

IT WAS NOW TWO AND A HALF YEARS since *Prince Robert* had been commissioned. There had been very few instances when her obsolete main armament had been fired in earnest. They had been fired many times in training. The ship had not met the ultimate test of engagement with an equal or superior enemy. But at no time in that period had Naval Service Headquarters been in any doubt that she should continue on indefinitely in a role for which she was ill equipped or that was quickly becoming outdated as the danger from German raiders abated.

The option to replace her old six-inch guns with new more modern versions could not be met from British production. Debate between the Ottawa and Admiralty staffs continued, with Ottawa favoring twin four-inch weapons capable of high angle anti-aircraft fire. This weapon, with a lighter shell, could be much more easily loaded on the rolling deck of an AMC and had the added advantage of being built in Canada. The Admiralty acquiesced and the original plan was to re-equip all three of the *Princes*. While their usefulness as AMCs was still not clear and the cost of new armament was factored in, the more useful change to troop carrying landing ships was proposed by the Chief of Naval Staff. Again Admiralty agreed. But it was also decided in Ottawa to continue with the plan to convert *Prince Robert* to an anti-aircraft cruiser while her two sisters would be converted to Landing Ships Infantry (Medium).

Prince Robert was taken out of commission at the end of 1942 stripped of her guns, shells and other equipment and stores, and taken to Burrard Dry Docks in Vancouver. For the next five months she was in the hands of the "Dockyard Mateys" as naval ratings always referred to civilian workers. Commander O.C.S. "Long Robbie" Robertson, and Lieutenant-Commander E.W. "Ted" Finch-Noyes in turn represented naval interest, during the work period. By end of April her first four-inch twin mounting had been installed.

The final weapons arrangement as completed during conversion had ten twin four-inch HA/LA Mark XXV guns, eight 2-pounder pompoms, and Oerlikon 20mm. The four-inch mountings were centre-line fitted with two forward and three aft. These made a marked change to her broadside appearance. A director and fire control were fitted as well as relatively modern radar that was suitable for detecting aircraft and to provide warning, surface detection and fire control according to the ship's radar officer, Bill Johnson. Her new function was reflective of a condition that was rapidly evolving at sea. Britain was now building cruisers whose sole purpose was to shoot down enemy aircraft to provide A/A defence to convoys and other ships. With the new threat from the air, four-inch guns that could fire at high angles were needed more than higher caliber guns for which there were few targets for a surface to surface battle.

*Times change and we change with them

The work was complex and the Admiralty plans did not always arrive when needed. With most of the ship's company drafted to other ships, this period did at least permit the shore authorities to find and train seamen and officers for the ship's new role. With the heavy concentration in lighter and newer guns, the need for a number of trained gunners had increased. But as usual with ships in dockyard hands all came together to permit the *Prince Robert* to recommission on 7 June 1943. The new Captain was A.M. Hope, RCN. Known as "Boomer" to his contemporaries, he was another graduate of the Royal Naval College of Canada 1914. His specialty was, appropriately, gunnery and he had served in a number of capital ships in the R.N.

Prince Robert on trials after conversion to an AA Cruiser Courtesy Maritime Museum of B.C.

Local trials and exercises were completed. One sailor remembered the depth charge trial that was followed by sending row boats out to collect the salmon that were killed. When all the stores were on board, *Prince Robert*, A/A cruiser, sailed for the East Coast on 29 July. By 9 August she was through the Panama Canal. A junior Paymaster Officer on board was George Herring. In 1999 he

Three Princes Armed

recalled life in the ship as they steamed for Scotland. He mentioned a Warrant Gunner who was too close to the recoil of a 4-inch gun and took the impact on his nose. In the Caribbean a canvas pool was rigged in which the men could relax. In the wardroom a grand piano was bolted to the deck, a survivor from *Robert*'s grander days. After a brief stop in Bermuda where she topped up with a load of bananas the ship crossed the Atlantic and made anchor off Greenock in the River Clyde.

She now had to pass the tests of fighting efficiency before she could go to sea and face the test of operations and potential enemy actions. Her gunnery conditions were examined by the staff of HMS *Excellent*, the Royal Navy's gunnery school. A number of improvements were required. If she were to fight against aircraft, her aircraft warning radar and plotting were inadequate. The newer type 291 radar set was installed. Six more Oerlikon guns were fitted, bringing the number of that type up to twelve. All of this took time and was not assisted by a local labour dispute in the dockyard. Another problem that required the ship to be placed in the floating dock was a punctured asdic dome. The ship took advantage of these delays to send men to various Royal Navy schools for training. By late October *Prince Robert* had passed work-ups and final inspection and was ready for orders.

Not every moment on board was serious. George Herring said that seven or eight of the officers had left pregnant wives in Canada. So the Wardroom installed a clothesline on which was placed paper diapers, each with the name of an officer. As word was received of a birth a smear of peanut butter was placed on the diaper.

Prince Robert was fortunate at this time to have as her Radar Officer Bill Johnson. After special training at the University of Toronto in a highly secret course of Radio Direction Finding he received further training in the Royal Navy ashore and afloat, where secrecy was also emphasized. In an interview many years later he recalled the sets that his ship needed in its new role as an A/A cruiser. He proudly recalled the men in his department on board, none of whom were Electrical Artificers. They were just trained operators, and he could recite most of them by name. Johnson's principal concern was that, having set up a primitive Operations Room on board, the Captain and the Gunnery officers were not trained in modern use of radar, and the Captain had a pre-war attitude which was not conducive to learning about new equipment. Bill said that his sets included a 291, a 293, a 285 for gunnery, a 282 for auto barrage against low flying aircraft, a 277 for calculating aircraft height, plus one other set for the Pom-Poms. Bill had acquired one set in England that had been destined for a Royal Navy cruiser that had been sunk. Bill was trained in both theory and hands-on operations. One officer described the ship as "a veritable radar laboratory." Bill had even tried to construct a "jammer" to counter the German radio controlled bomb. The ship's Gunnery Officer was a Toronto based pre-war Naval Reservist, Lieutenant-Commander Robert I. Hendy, a lawyer who was to spend his whole adult life in the Reserves, retiring post war as a Commodore.

The sea war had changed dramatically from the 1940 scene when *Prince Robert* had first commissioned. Then the enemy consisted of battle cruisers, armed merchant raiders and German ships attempting to run the blockade home with needed supplies. Gradually the U-boat menace had become critical, with wolf packs taking a large toll from some of the convoys. That balance had ebbed and flowed as each side found new naval and air tactics and better equipment. The Allies improved their under water detection equipment and were adding new forms of depth bombs. Long range aircraft were closing the gaps between North America and Europe. The Germans were developing "schnorkel" and were putting more anti-aircraft guns on their submarines. By May of 1943 there was a turn of the anti-U-boat tide. Admiral Doenitz was faced with the appalling loss of forty of his fleet of U-boats in that one month. Twelve of these were sunk in the first week of May alone including

U 439 that collided with U 659, sinking both. Five were sunk in one battle against convoy ONS5. Doenitz recalled his U boats from the Atlantic.

By the fall of 1943 Doenitz had countered the Allied advantages with new radar detection systems which provided his captains some ability to avoid being attacked without some warning and with "schnorkel" to allow operations submerged to avoid aircraft detection. The submarines were assisted by new long-range aircraft, mostly Focke-Wulf 200 Condors, to find targets for submarines and to home them to the convoys. The German aircraft were also intended to attack convoys and could do so from long range with the newly developed glider-bomb. Many of the convoys were now destined for the Mediterranean where the allies were fighting the Germans in Italy and where the large armies required support from the sea. The convoy routes brought them closer to German detection devices and to attacking aircraft. Those convoys needed ships that could counter air attacks, and *Prince Robert* was assigned to Gibraltar so that she could be part of the defence of convoys running between the United Kingdom and the Mediterranean. It was one of the more dangerous areas in the sea war and the Germans were just then exerting an increasing pressure on the convoys. Among the new weapons being used was the Heinkel 177 aircraft carrying two rocket assisted flying bombs which could be directed by the control aircraft from a distance. These were in addition to Junkers 88 and Focke-Wulf 200s. And of course the submarine menace was ever present.

One of the officers who joined *Prince Robert* in October 1943 was Lieutenant Dacre Cole, RCNVR. He was the third assistant gunnery officer, and in "Salty Dips" Volume 6 he described the four-inch guns as "noisy little things, awfully sharp crack. They were terrible. They would occasionally blow smoke rings too." He recalled that "we went to the Med in late 1943 and it was relatively quiet at that time. We had some dive bomb attacks in the Bay of Biscay and we went out to meet a convoy that was being attacked by Heinkel 177s. We went through to Gib, and sometimes to Naples, picked up a convoy coming back there." He also noted that they did go back with convoys to Plymouth and even to Belfast when all the southern ports were full of vessels destined for the invasion landings in Normandy. Cole was however most grateful for the luxurious accommodation that he found on board. He had previously served in the British corvette HMS *Bluebell* in the North Sea, and a liner type cabin was a pleasant improvement.

Officers of Prince Robert as identified by Lieutenant Harold Moist in 1986. 1st row – MacMillan, Calhoun, Atwood, Hope, Bulmer, Hendy, La Couvee. 2nd row – Clayton, Fricke, Sexsmith, Newell, NK, Johnson, Hager, Birtwhistle, Koyle, Gravelle. 3rd row – Wallace, NK, Mau, Freeman, Moist, Dieble, Hayward. 4th row – NK, NK, NK, Hibbert, Cole, Dannigan NK, NK Photo courtesy Bill Johnson

Three Princes Armed

Prince Robert's officers by now were almost all RCNVR, reflecting the maturity of reservists as the war progressed. The captain was RCN and some of the engineers were RCNR. Strangely, according to the February 1944 Canadian Navy List the wardroom numbers had swelled to 33 officers from the 22 on commissioning. Conversely, the March 1945 edition of that book showed that the wardroom was back to 22 officers. Harold Moist had moved from the Chief Petty Officers' mess to the wardroom where he was the sole RCNVR Commissioned Boatswain serving in the navy.

Lieutenant (Special Branch) Peter MacRitchie, a Public Relations Officer on board, noted that so many men of the ship's company had changed that there were just six left who had commissioned *Prince Robert* in July 1940. Besides Moist they were Chief Engine Room Artificer R. Lang, Chief Stoker Petty Officer W. Kerry, Chief Electrical Artificer M.D. Butt, Able Seaman D. Pritchard a quartermaster, and Able Seaman G.F. Hill, the Canteen Manager. MacRitchie calculated that these men had traveled almost 200,000 miles in their ship.

Prince Robert now entered this active scene of action for duty as an A/A Cruiser protecting convoys from air attack. Malcolm Macleod described the general system as follows. "Fast Convoys between the United Kingdom and North Africa were designated KMF and MKF. Their cycle was thirty-five days, and *Prince Robert* shuttled back and forth between Plymouth and Gibraltar with them. On the run outward from Great Britain the anti-aircraft cruiser was usually ordered to sail from Plymouth thirty hours or so before making rendezvous with the convoy, which had entered the Atlantic via the Northwest Approaches north of Ireland. The meeting place was about two hundred miles west of that island. Anti-submarine escort vessels, five or six in number, usually sailed from Londonderry. At the other end, until June 1944, Gibraltar was *Prince Robert*'s turn-about port whence other forces took up the protection of the vessels that were proceeding eastward into the Mediterranean." Some convoys originating in Sierra Leone, designated SL, joined up with the UK/ North Africa convoys.

Robert's captain described how his ship operated when with a convoy. He placed his ship generally on the land side of the convoy, sometimes in an outer screen some five miles away, and if the convoy was to come under threat of air attack, he would move to within the convoy itself. Action Stations was the normal condition from first light until sunset.

Prince Robert arrived at Gibraltar on 24th October 1943. Her first convoy was MKF25 which contained a number of troopship liners including the Canadian Pacific *Duchess of Bedford*. On board the liners were 60,000 passengers including women and children. Some were Allied prisoners of war who had been recaptured. Peter MacRitchie noted that the presence of so many of those who had suffered in the war created a special sense of responsibility among the men of the *Robert*. The gunners saw their first enemy aircraft, but it was at too great a distance for action. So their first convoy arrived unscathed in early November.

Her next stop from 4 to 11 November was in the Azores, where the ship's company had a few days of relaxation, sports and shopping. On 16th November they were back in the UK. On the 20th she sailed to help relieve the combined convoy SL139/MKS30 headed north. That large group of ships was under attack from numerous submarines and the authorities felt that air attack would soon follow. For *Prince Robert* the battle in which she was to participate was to be the most singular action of her whole service career where her armament played the principal role.

The convoy of 67 ships had actually been detected by the Germans as early as 16 November. By the 18th the action with the gathering submarines had begun. The first ship struck was the British ship *Chanticleer* of 1,350 tons. *U 515* under KL Werner Henke damaged her with a torpedo, but *Chanticleer* was later towed to port. Retribution was quick. On the 19th *U 211* was destroyed with all hands by an RAF Wellington from 179 Squadron based in the Azores. The pilot was D.M. McRae, RCAF, his third success.

Canadian surface units at this point in the war were also becoming accomplished in the skills of anti-submarine warfare. The kill of *U 211* was followed the next day by ships from a Canadian Support Group. The frigate HMCS *Nene* first had a radar contact and in a chase the submarine dived. Contact was gained by the corvettes HMCS *Snowberry*, joined by HMCS *Calgary* and the *Nene* in punishing depth charge attacks. When *U 536* was blown to the surface, three officers and 14 sailors were rescued by the Canadians, whilst 38 others perished. One of the authors recalls a veteran of HMCS *Nene* in college after the war who said "We pulled the German men on board by their watch straps." The submarine sank at 0247 AM. *Snowberry* and *Calgary* were given credit for the kill. On the 21st another U-boat was killed by the frigate HMS *Foley* and the sloop HMS *Crane* of Support Group SG7. *U 538* was sunk with all 55 of its crew.

With the first phase over and the balance in favor of the convoy escort, the Germans now threw in their aircraft. En route to join the escort *Prince Robert* detected two Focke-Wulf 200s on the radar set, and exercised her four-inch guns at long range. Over the convoy a large group of Focke-Wulf and Heinkel aircraft were attacking. Some of the ships claimed hits as they fired their anti-aircraft weapons. One ship was a straggler and suffered the all too frequent straggler fate, and was sunk by bombs.

Prince Robert could see much of the action as she steamed at full speed to bring her armament within range. On joining the escort she immediately took on a German who was attacking the corvette HMCS *Lunenburg*. Firing everything in her weapons suite she filled the air with bursting shells. What followed was an hour of almost continuous firing that stands out in the memories of the veterans of the action as shell casings from the 4-inch piled up around the five mounts. In the words of seaman Jack Aldred years later, "I remember we were firing the guns for quite a while, we had so many empty shell casings laying around we had to kick them over the side to make room to move around. It was our first taste of action and it was just steady going, just the way we'd practiced. All we could see were specks up in the sky as we approached the convoy that was under attack. We just sailed in with "all guns blazing". I didn't realize it lasted two hours, but as I say, we were just firing away, the way we'd trained over and over to do. Up until a couple of years ago I didn't feel our ship had done much, after listening to my brother tell about subs and the North Atlantic, but I met an old school chum who had been on one of the corvettes escorting the convoy that was under attack, and he told me how glad they were to see the *Robert* come roaring in like the cavalry in a western movie, it made me feel a little better." And through it all Peter MacRitchie, the Public Relations Officer, was describing action over the ship's broadcast system for those whose stations kept them in the ship's interior.

Prince Robert sailors painting ship at Gibraltar Author's collection

Three Princes Armed

The merchant ship *Delius* was the next ship to be struck by bombs, but her crew was able to keep their ship afloat. The efforts of *Prince Robert* caused her to be singled out by three German aircraft. Two of them were beaten off before they could release their bombs. One appeared to be well lined up with its bomb propulsion engine flashing red. Apparently the release mechanism did not work and the German flew off with the red light still flashing. They watched from the bridge of *Robert* as the aircraft finally got rid of its bomb aimed at a freighter. Amazed, they saw the bomb run at the ship then turn upward between the ship's mast only to crash in the sea. To the men of *Prince Robert* this introduction to all-out attack and defense left them with a sense of great pride in their ability to accomplish what their ship was designed for and they were trained for. The results in terms of aircraft damaged or destroyed were inconclusive. None crashed within sight of the convoy. But three HE177s did not make it back to their stations. Most importantly, the action accomplished what escorts were meant to do. That was, the safe return of the ships being escorted. And there is no doubt that *Prince Robert* contributed effectively to the achievement of that goal.

Ceremony of the Keys, Gibraltar Author's collection

By late November in company with a convoy *Robert* was back in Plymouth where she began almost a full year of running with convoys. Except for the times in Plymouth where, linked by land lines to the port's defences, her guns fired at German aircraft over the city, at no time did she have to fire her guns in anger at the enemy while at sea. She accompanied seventeen convoys. From 10 December 1943 until June of 1944 her route was Gibraltar to UK with Plymouth, Greenock and Belfast as the northern turnaround ports. From June until mid September her southern terminus was Naples. The ship saw much sea time but no action. The sailors were aware of possible enemy aircraft or submarines every time they sailed so they could not relax at sea. One might argue that the sight of a well armed anti-aircraft escorts encouraged the enemy to look elsewhere for less forbidding targets. Time in port relieved the tensions of convoy escort. Sailors have a way of making the most of their leave ashore in a foreign port and to some of them every port is a foreign port.

In March of 1944, while in Gibraltar, *Robert* provided an Honour Guard for the ancient Ceremony of the Keys, a rare event for a Commonwealth country. This ceremony dates back to 1779 when the French and Spanish were trying to invade the Rock. It symbolizes the guard locking the four gates at night. Today the Guard marches the Port Sergeant to one of the gates and the keys are returned to the Governor during an official dinner that night. *Prince Robert's* last convoy was MKF 34 that brought her to Plymouth. She had been away from Canada for many months and there were now many new ships to take her place on convoy escort duties. It was agreed between the Admiralty and Ottawa that it was time for her to return to Canada.

Prince Robert sailed for Esquimalt arriving there on 12 October 1944. Most of the ship's company were granted long leave, and the ship placed in Care and Maintenance condition. Anticipating possible service in the ongoing Pacific war in December she was paid off to undergo refit in Vancouver. Of course the whole question of her employment was initiated by naval staff. They were not approving large sums of money until her future role was decided. The decision was taken that she should remain as an anti-aircraft ship and as such certain improvements to her armament, radar and plotting equipment were also approved. Changes were inevitably made to the original plan and *Robert* was not ready until early June 1945. Over one million dollars had been spent to make *Robert* a more effective fighting ship. With the collapse of Japan seemingly imminent it is difficult to understand the thinking in Ottawa although at that time it was thought that the war would drag on into 1946. The nuclear bombs were still very secret when Ottawa planners were making decisions. When the war ended the ship did not fit into Headquarters' plans for the post-war navy. Planners in Ottawa envisioned a relatively strong force of modern cruisers and destroyers.

Regardless of post-war planning, *Robert* was ready and available and had proved her worth as an anti-aircraft cruiser. When she departed Esquimalt to join the British Task Group 111.2, the

Captain W.B. Creery Courtesy F.W. Bryan, Winnipeg

Japanese Kamikaze aircraft were still a major threat and *Robert's* guns were a useful addition to the war. Canada was obviously anxious to be a participant in the events unfolding in the Pacific war. Both of the cruisers newly acquired from the Royal Navy, HMCS *Uganda* and HMCS *Ontario*, had been directed to join the British forces in the Pacific. Of course, very few knew in July 1945 that the atom bomb was to bring about the early collapse of Japan.

Rum issue on board Library and Archives Canada PR 536

US Commodore being piped on board Prince Robert, San Francisco Library and Archives Canada PR 337

Three Princes Armed

In the very controversial decision by Ottawa to ask all sailors to vote for discharge or continuing in service until Japan was defeated, the *Prince Robert* sailors later voted 85% on carrying on. This was greatly to the satisfaction of the new captain. The same encouraging result had not been voted in *Uganda*.

On 4 June 1945 *Prince Robert* commissioned under Captain Wallace Creery, RCN. He was a graduate of the 5th term from Royal Naval College of Canada. Prior to the war he qualified as a Torpedo specialist. He was Commanding Officer of the destroyer HMCS *Fraser* when that ship was run down and sunk by the British cruiser HMS *Calcutta* in June of 1940 off the French coast, and he retired as a Rear Admiral in 1955.

On board weapons training for landing party Library and Archives Canada PR 406

After the usual work-ups *Robert* was ready to join the operations against Japan. The "usual" workups included gun function trials in the Straits of Juan da Fuca just off Peddar Bay. One of the

Landing Party at Hong Kong Library and Archives Canada PR 412

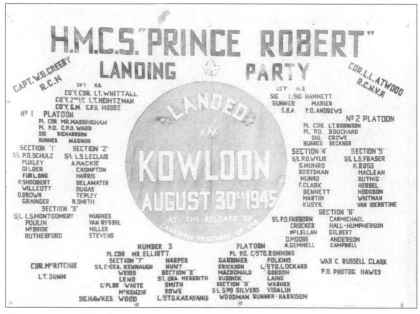

Composition of landing party Courtesy Bill Johnson

Three Princes Armed

loading numbers of the left gun of "Q" mounting was Ordinary Seaman Phil Bissell, who recalled the event in the Naval Officer's Association newsletter many years later as the "Tweed Curtain Caper." As his gun's turn came to fire salvoes of five rounds his gun captain informed the bridge that it was an unsafe bearing. The bridge replied "Concern yourself with safety and we will worry about safe bearing" "Q" mounting commenced firing. When the bridge saw that there was no splash where it should be the Check Fire bell was sounded. A Mr. Olson of 1101 Beach Drive in Oak Bay was relaxing in his garden when he heard a whining sound and saw a splash just yards off his shoreline. The second round landed even closer. He and his family ran for shelter. Golfers at Victoria Golf Club were also concerned about the noise of passing shells. The Navy managed to cover the incident by wartime secrecy of ship's movements. *Prince Robert* sailed from Esquimalt on 4 July.

Her first port was San Francisco where she was directed to replace her four twin Oerlikon guns with four single heavier caliber and more effective Bofors. This delayed the planned sailing date from 11 July until the 20th. Creery took the opportunity to have his men receive damage control training with the USN. The threat of Japanese "Kamikaze" aircraft may have been in his mind. His Report of Proceedings for the period ending 10th August reveals that his planned duties "were to provide additional A.A. support for the Light Fleet Carriers." En route to Pearl Harbor all the guns were exercised and the ship arrived at that now historic port on 26 July. They sailed again on the 28th and arrived in Sydney, Australia on 10 August where they joined Task Group 111.2 under Rear Admiral Harcourt RN in the aircraft carrier HMS *Indomitable*. Two days later the ship's company learned that Japan had capitulated. This meant that the new duties of the Task Group were the enforcement of surrender terms and release of prisoners of war.

The end of the shooting war led to a rather bizarre comment by the ship's Medical Officer. In his routine report he suggested that the Executive Branch officers on board were "distressed" because they would not have a chance to see more action. Creery said later that he would have taken exception to that comment had he read it more carefully at the time. He emphasized that all officers and sailors would not want to risk their own lives or those of others.

The following coverage of the events that transpired is taken from a number of sources. Firstly Malcolm Macleod's paper is as always a prime source. Admiral Creery not only provided copies of his Reports of Proceedings but he also corresponded with author Fraser McKee in 1970 with more details. Numerous messages among the ships in the Task Group are quoted. These were provided by the Naval & Military Museum in Esquimalt and give some immediacy to the narrative. Some of the participants gave their stories and photographs.

The route of the Task group took them from Manus in the Admiralty Islands, part of Papua New Guinea, then on to Leyte in the Philippines. On the 29th of August the Task Group anchored north of Tam Kan Island, 12 miles from Hong Kong. They were in company with HMS *Maidstone* a submarine depot ship and seven Australian minesweepers. In his Report of Proceedings Creery said that as the rain cleared, Stanley Prison, where the Japanese had interned civilian prisoners, was in view.

Message from Commander Task Group: "*My intentions tomorrow are to transfer to SWIFTSURE (cruiser) and proceed into Hong Kong with EURYALUS (cruiser), PRINCE ROBERT, KEMPENFELT (destroyer), URSA (submarine) and two submarines ordered by SM8. If passage is made without incident MAIDSTONE (submarine depot ship) and other submarines will be called in. If that is successful ANSON (battleship) and INDOMITABLE (aircraft carrier) will also enter. Minesweepers will continue sweeping. ANSON with TYRIAN (destroyer) will be detached to anchor north of Tam Kan and BS1 is requested to coordinate sailing of ships from that anchorage. It is considered that the risk of suicides is not small.*" This arrangement developed after Admiral Harcourt had been in touch with the local Japanese commander by radio and the commander's representative had been flown to the flagship by an aircraft from *Indomitable*.

The feelings on board *Prince Robert* are difficult to imagine. The size of the naval armada alone gave a sense of magnitude and awe to the proceedings. Minesweepers were about their deadly business reminding all of undersea dangers even within the harbour of Hong Kong. Aircraft were constantly overhead from the carriers. Some were dropping medical supplies to the camps but others were looking for suicide craft. The Japanese had not formally surrendered (the official surrender was signed on board USS *Missouri* on 2 September with regional surrenders in Singapore and Penang being signed days later) and no one really knew whether the troops would obey the local commanders. Captain Creery was the senior Canadian in the area and his feelings of responsibility to his ship

Able Seaman Paul Shoobert on shore patrol with a Japanese soldier Library and Archives Canada PR 410

and men was mixed with a sense of pride in the mission and its safe accomplishment. The intensity on the bridge was palpable.

Message from CTG 111.4 to *ANSON* and *PRINCE ROBERT*: *"I shall probably ask you to be responsible for law and order on the Kowloon side using landing parties from ANSON and PR for this purpose. Am berthing PR alongside at Kowloon. The establishment of town patrols will be in order to maintain law and order. Patrols are to be guided by the following rules (A) The Japanese have not yet surrendered and will not do so until the surrender is signed in Tokyo. There may therefore still be armed Japanese patrols about but they should not be molested unless they are disturbing the peace. (B) All other persons carrying arms are to be arrested and disarmed. Looters and rioters may be shot but rather they should be arrested so they may be brought to trial. A great deal will depend on the bearing and attitude of our patrols. They are to be particularly alert at all times."*

Naval ships have traditionally provided shore patrols in port where the most serious problem they deal with are fellow shipmates who have had too much to drink and become obstreperous. Hong Kong was not something they had been trained for. They had no local intelligence to prepare them for the kind of reception they would receive. To convey the Commander's desires and rules in the short time before landing must have placed a heavy burden on the Captain and those officers who led the patrols. It says much for the intelligence and flexibility of the Canadians that they took to this unfamiliar role with ease. They went ashore in three platoons totaling 91 men.

Captain Creery's Report next describes his entry into Kowloon. "HMCS *Prince Robert* therefore steamed at slow speed past the waterfront of Kowloon giving careful inspection to the various wharves. Holt's Wharf presented the advantage of being clearly within visual signaling touch of the flagship and easily guarded and therefore selected. To the accompaniment of shrieks of joy from the Chinese onlookers *Prince Robert* made fast to Holt's Wharf at

1330, 30th August 1945." The shore platoons were immediately landed. The bridge had observed that at the extension of the wharf a small coastal steamer and a barge were being loaded by armed Japanese soldiers. Some of the items being loaded were judged to be loot. Three platoons had been landed. Lieutenant Whittal was the Company Commander and he was instructed to carry out a reconnaissance of the area in the vicinity of the wharf. No 3 Platoon was given the task of securing the wharf and the adjacent warehouses to prevent possible sniping.

Unfortunately the number 2 platoon commander, the Gunner, Mr. Massington, slipped on a small stone wall which caused his Sten gun to discharge a round, striking him in the left upper arm. He was taken back on board and later taken to Australia for treatment.

Message from *Prince Robert* to Commander Task Group: *"Area at present secured from railway station to east of boats wharf. Wharf abreast of railway station was only taken over after looting by Chinese commenced. Only arms confiscated were from Japanese soldiers loading ship at Holt's Wharf. Am stopping all loading of food on Japanese ships."*

Captain Creery commented years later on the fact that his men had disarmed some of the Japanese. In an article Creery wrote and in Malcolm MacLeod's paper the event was described. "Actually it was contrary to an agreement made with the Japanese commander on board *Indomitable* the previous day, since they were to be responsible for the maintenance of civil order until the British could muster a large force to take over this responsibility. However they were loading a coastal vessel or two with various kinds of loot and I made a quick decision to deal with this breach of the agreement by making one myself. This was deeply resented by the Japanese officer in command of the troops in that area and we eyed each other steadily for a moment or two. Whether or not he was influenced by the fact that I had a large Able Seaman beside me who was poking a Tommy gun into his belly, I wouldn't know but

Prince Robert sailors shopping for souvenirs Library and Archives Canada PR 507

I felt considerably relieved when he hissed, saluted and gave the necessary orders for the troops to disarm." Years later Creery added these additional comments. " He then proceeded towards a waiting car when I informed him that all the cars had been commandeered. At which point he shrugged and departed."

Message from *Prince Robert* to CTG: *"Have cleared immediate dock area of Japanese. There is a definite danger that the Japanese will withdraw their patrols from the city and minor cases of looting have already taken place. I am marching a small force through the streets in the vicinity but will be unable to control looting if it breaks out on a large scale. Have commandeered arms, motor cars and trucks found on the wharf."*

Message from CTG to *Prince Robert*: *"Well Done."*

Message from CTF to all ships: *"Boats which may be suicides* reported leaving Picnic Bay. All ships to be on the alert. They should be attacked." Malcolm Macleod said that some of these suicide craft loaded with explosives did try to get underway but were destroyed by bombing.

Captain Creery summarized this portion of the action in his Report. He said that his men had acted with initiative and suitable dignity and were a credit. They were cool and steady in the face of vastly superior numbers of Japanese soldiers. They did not take advantage of their position by looting or collecting souvenirs. Later when his men had fewer responsibilities, Creery did have some concerns about some of his people.

The fate of the prisoners of war became the important issue. Camp Sham Shui Po was the camp where some 1500 British, Canadian and Allied prisoners were held. Of these 68 officers and 302 other ranks were Canadians. In May 1957 Peter MacRitchie wrote in the Naval Officer's of Canada Journal some memories of his visit to the camp. He wrote "My chief function was to find the Canadian prisoners, so after taking part in the preliminary round-up, I made my way to the main street, Nathan Avenue, where the ravenous coolies had taken matters into their own hands and were busy looting Japanese food trucks. If you have never seen coolies looting, you sure have missed something. It's the most systematic operation this side of the Styx.

Camp Sham Shui Po was barely two miles from where *Prince Robert* lay. I found it through the good guidance of a White Russian girl, who overjoyed at being liberated, bundled me into a ricksha and set off at a spanking pace. What a surprise was in store for me. I had expected that the Canadian repatriation officials, bound from Chunking, had preceded me to the camp. But travel by air was rather difficult. So that, along with the ship's photographer. I was the first to get there, and what a good old-fashioned Canadian whoop rent the air at the sight of our "Canada" shoulder badges. Conditions at Sham Shui Po could not help but improve. Food was better, but the days of waiting for that one word that spells HOME seemed interminable, longer the boys said, than all the forty-four months they had spent as prisoners. And, so finally, after herding a Japanese nondescript regiment behind these same wire entanglements the survivors of Canada's ill-fated brigade went home. But before their departure they were the constant guests of the officers and men of *Prince Robert*. Captain Creery saw to it that their welfare was paramount. And I see them now, marching through that unspeakable barrier of barbed wire at Sham Shui Po on that far off Sunday morning en route for embarkation in the *Empress of Australia*. Skinny and bronzed, their heads high, arms swinging, they were roundly cheered by their camp mates of other nations, themselves waiting for the long voyage home."

Released Canadian prisoner with Prince Robert sailors Library and Archives Canada PR 413

MacRitchie also filed a report to the Canadian Broadcasting Company in which he told of some of the prisoners that he met. Included were Lieutenant John Park of the Winnipeg Grenadiers, Private John James also of the Grenadiers, Lieutenants Frank Power and Doug Johnson of the Royal Rifles. They said that they had had barely enough to subsist on. One part of the diet was called The Green Horror in the camp. It was mostly the tubular stem of watercress. The Japanese were indifferent to the prisoners' sickness and did not pass all the contents of Red Cross parcels to the men.

The camps were not guarded by the Japanese. The guards had been removed on 15 August. The fact that the first of the releasing force to arrive at the camp were Canadians was assessed as having a beneficial psychological effect on the prisoners. They were found to have a high standard of morale, reasonably good physical condition, were well disciplined and anxious for information on world affairs. Any judgment of the conditions of the prisoners at that early stage would fail to take into account the long-term effects of malnutrition and the psychological impact of extended incarceration under inhuman treatment by the captors.

Being free to move about, some of the prisoners went on board *Robert* where some found relatives and old friends. The ship's company were generous with boots and everything else of possible use including chocolate bars. The ship also arranged to have items sent to the camp so that as many of the prisoners as possible would receive some benefits. Captain Creery took some of the prisoners on board where space permitted and his regret was that his ability to accommodate more was so limited.

The Canadian shore patrols continued, with the sailors moving further into town. They began to appreciate that their problems were not so much with the Japanese but with the local Chinese, many of whom were looting. The shore patrols caught a number of them and locked them up. Royal Marines were brought in to help maintain order.

One officer took full advantage of his time in Hong Kong. Bill Johnson's interest in radar drew him up a hill to a Japanese radar site. He was able to examine it sufficiently that he could produce reports on their capabilities. He felt that they were inferior to British sets. Interviewed in Victoria many years later he still had photos and copies of his reports.

The ship's medical report made interesting and entertaining reading. In addition to the usual comments about the general health of those on board, the conditions in the mess-decks, the need for better air conditioning to combat the heat and the food, the Doctor observed in Hong Kong. "A most satisfactory attitude is seen in the men's conduct ashore. They don't drink water and they don't eat food, except bananas, although they do use spirits and beer freely and have suffered no decline in their libido." The Doctor and his staff had their hands full later when the ship took on board the soldiers and missionary passengers in Manila. Their medical conditions varied, as did the mental attitudes of some of them. In his final report Captain Creery singled out his Principal Medical Officer Acting Surgeon Lieutenant-Commander John W. Hackney, RCNVR, for his compassionate, careful and thorough treatment of the repatriates.

Although some of the men were in relatively good condition, it was apparent that this situation was of recent conditions and probably due to the Japanese captors and the prisoners recognizing that the day of reckoning was fast approaching. Their daily rations had consisted mainly of rice. Over the three years and eight months of captivity many had died from starvation and other elements of the treatment they had suffered. Lieutenant-Colonel E.E. Denison listed the names of the Royal Rifles who died in the camps. He said that 107 Canadians died at Sham Shui Po from 26 September 1942 until 1 September 1945. Another 22 died at North Point, another Camp near by in Hong Kong, in the nine months they were there. The survivors had the satisfaction before they left Hong Kong of seeing their old captors being marched into the same camp that had been the location of their long period of misery.

The two full battalions and support elements that had landed in Hong Kong in December of 1941 numbered 1,975. When *Robert* arrived in August of 1945 that total had been reduced by those who were killed in the action prior to surrender. Those who were not killed spent the first year in the Hong Kong camps. Lance Corporal Larry Stebbe was a member of the Winnipeg Grenadiers. He was very sick with diphtheria in the first months. Many years later he described how the selection was made of the approximately 750 who were taken to Japan and forced to work, some in the Mitsubishi shipyards, and others in the coal mines or other places. He said that in January 1943 all the Canadians except those in hospital with beriberi and palagra as well as most of the officers were lined up on one side of the road that ran through the camp. The soldiers were then ordered to cross the street. They were not told why. Approximately 750 were able to cross without the aid of crutches or stumbling. They were the "able" ones who were shipped off to Japan as slave labour.

Not all the prisoners were forcefully taken to Tokyo. John Stroud had originally joined the Toronto Scottish Regiment. Seeking adventure and action he transferred to the Royal Rifles of Canada when he found that his regiment was not slated for immediate overseas duty. He arrived in Hong Kong on board the *Awatea*. After being taken prisoner he was moved to North Point Camp. At North Point the prisoners were forced to build a runway. They were overjoyed when a VIP aircraft went through the runway on landing and nosed over. When he heard that some prisoners were going to Japan he thought things would be better there and he was able to join them. He later realized his mistake. Things were just as bad at the new location. Their Red Cross parcels were stolen, and they were fed and treated badly. He lost 100 pounds during his period as a prisoner. The remaining 450 prisoners stayed in Hong Kong.

Of those who went to Japan, 136 died. Four who remained were shot after escaping and recapture. By the time *Robert* arrived the Hong Kong group had been further reduced by 170 deaths. The Canadians left 557 soldiers in the graves of Asia.

Captain Creery's next Report of Proceedings covered the period from 1 September until 26 September. On the 3rd *Robert* moved from Holt's Wharf to No. 1 Wharf, Kowloon. The reduction in formal duties for the ship brought some bad behavior in a small number of the sailors. The Captain felt that this was caused by the long period without leave and the let down after the excitement of the first few days in Hong Kong. To see the Royal Navy and Royal Marines take over the duties that they had done so well was viewed with displeasure by the proud Canadians. Creery asked the authorities to assign his ship some further duties and they responded by having him anchor his ship off Stonecutter's Island where he would guard the magazine area. The ship was moved on the 6th. He was relieved of that duty on the 8th and directed to accompany the *Empress of Australia* to an anchorage to superintend the embarkation of internees from Stanley Camp. All the occupants of Sham Shui

Normal routine included deck scrubbing Author's collection

Po, including most of the Canadians, were among those taken on board the liner. The *Empress of Australia* sailed for Sydney on the 11th, the same day that HMCS *Ontario*, Canada's newest cruiser, arrived at Hong Kong.

The formal ceremony of surrender next occupied Captain Creery and the other senior military personnel. There was some early indecision as to who would be the actual signers from the Allied side. Captain Grant of *Ontario* was senior to Captain Creery but Admiral Harcourt insisted that Creery would represent Canada at the formal ceremony. When all the niceties of diplomacy had been concluded, on Sunday 16 September 1945, Creery and Brigadier Kay, Canadian Military Attache, were two of the immediate witnesses to the signing.

Prince Robert now was no longer needed, and after some fleet reorganization was released from any further duties. She sailed for

Prince Robert securing at Esquimalt jetty with ex-prisoners on B gun deck
Courtesy Naval and Military Museum, Esquimalt

Manila on the 26th where she took on board six officers and 50 other ranks, ex-prisoners of war and some missionaries, for passage to Canada via Pearl Harbor. Manila was a very crowded anchorage, and the arrangements for taking the passengers on board were not helped by bad communications between the ship and the Naval Liaison ashore. In rough weather they embarked them from a US landing craft, and sailed late in the evening which helped them to just avoid a typhoon that struck the coast of Luzon the next day.

Their reception at Pearl Harbour was most generous. It included support from the Red Cross and a cable company that came on board and accepted cables from the passengers to their homes without charging for them.

But it was the reception in the Dockyard at Esquimalt on the 20th October that was the highlight of the return journey. Creery described it as overwhelming. In addition to the band playing and the ship's sirens hooting, it was the cheering of the crowds filling the jetties that was so moving. It was mainly the fact that these ex-prisoners were able to be repatriated by a Canadian warship that added luster to the occasion.

Malcolm Macleod very aptly summed up *Prince Robert*'s relationship with the soldiers of the Winnipeg Grenadiers and Quebec's Royal Rifles of Canada, "The connection imposes a definite unity upon her entire far-flung career as a man-of-war. Early, she brought the Canadian soldiers to an ambush, a battle glorious in disaster, their alternatives death or despair. Now the selfsame ship, so far from home, and so long afterwards, returns to rescue the survivors from debilitating incarceration."

This is essentially the story of three warships. But the "unity" that Macleod refers to is one that has no end. The prisoners who returned to Canada had many stories. For many it was a relatively early death from the decreased health that they suffered. Others had successful lives but never outlived their experiences while in the camps. One of those was Kenneth Cambon, a 17 year old

Private of the Royal Rifles of Canada. After the war he became a successful Doctor and wrote of his 44 months, much of it in Camp 5B in Niigata, Japan. In his "Guest of Hirohito" he said he would never return to Japan. But he relented after his daughter had gone there and was told the camp never existed. When he demanded the truth from the city the mayor apologized. So in 1989 he returned and was honoured as the first of the camp inmates to do so. He visited the coal yards where he had been forced to work. He was treated with warmth and hospitality. Ken Cambon died in 2007 pleased that reconciliation was possible.

HMCS *Prince Robert's* time as a warship had now come to an end. The men who had sailed her at the end were quickly drafted ashore, many of them, the Reserves, to begin release proceedings from the navy. The ship paid off on 10 December 1945 and on 18 January 1946 she became the property of War Assets Corporation for disposal.

CHAPTER FIVE

Operation Neptune

We shall fight on the beaches, we shall fight on the landing grounds,
we shall fight in the fields and in the streets—

Churchill June 1940

IN EARLY 1943 OTTAWA TOOK THE DECISION to convert *Prince David* and *Prince Henry* to Landing Ships Infantry (Medium). Ottawa also insisted that the work of conversion be carried out in Canada even though Burrard Dry Dock, the chosen contractor, could not carry out all the changes necessary to finish the job. The yard had undertaken the conversion of *Prince Robert*, which delayed some work on the other two, so the two sister ships did not pay off until the end of April 1943.

Because some of the specialized equipment could only be completed in the UK it was not until just before Christmas that *Prince David* could be recommissioned. Her new Captain was Commander T.D. "Doug" Kelly, RCNR. Kelly was an experienced mariner. He had trained in sailing ships and had been with Imperial Oil tankers for many years. In 1932, when he was Master of the *Ontariolite*, he accepted the post of Harbour Master in Talara, Peru. The men who sailed with him all held him in high esteem as an excellent ship handler. *David* sailed and spent her first Christmas as a LSI (Medium) at sea, between Esquimalt and Balboa en route the Panama Canal. The diary of ERA Jimmy Kaufman (post-war

Doctor James O. Kaufman) noted a rough passage with many of those on board rushing for the lee rails (known in the Navy as "calling for Bill"). The ship made good time and arrived in New York on 9 January 1945.

Meanwhile *Prince Henry* was just days behind. The new Commanding Officer of *Henry* was Captain Val Godfrey, RCN, who had returned to *Prince* ships having commanded *Prince David* from December 1941 to April 1943. Unlike Kelly who was at ease on the bridge, Godfrey was described by at least one of his officers as "a real gentleman but not a great ship handler. Very nervous and uptight when entering harbour and took a long time to come alongside." Kelly had served with him for a brief period so the two captains were well acquainted. Godfrey's new LSI(M) commissioned on 4 January 1944 and sailed immediately.

Malcolm Macleod described the two ships as they left Esquimalt for the continuing war. "Even at this stage of their conversion the two *Prince* ships' appearance had been altered beyond compare with any other vessel in the thirty-four years of the Royal Canadian Navy. On each ship, a row of huge davits ran half the length port and starboard. Each pair was capable of lifting twenty tons from the sea. Later they would hold stubby little landing craft, an outfit of eight per ship"

There were other changes. The obsolete six-inch and three-inch guns were removed, perhaps to find appropriate homes in naval or military museums. The anti-submarine equipment was left for whatever possible use could have been imagined. The ship did get some new useful four-inch High/Low angle guns; two twin mountings. To these were added eight single Oerlikons and two 40 mm guns.

The interior of each ship was greatly altered, recognizing her new role of carrying and landing up to 450 soldiers complete with weapons and packs. Housekeeping changes included large mess-decks served by a cafeteria, and expanded storerooms for the necessities of life. Malcolm Macleod reported that, (much like today's sailors, who have christened the central passageways with names like "Burma Road" and the Main Street names of the City class frigates,) the Prince ships dubbed these large spaces as "The Ritz", "Dirty Dick's" and "Chez Maurice." Macleod also said that *Prince Henry* managed to accommodate 1700 passengers complete with their weapons and baggage on one occasion.

The dictionary defines "Amphibious" as "capable of surviving on both land and sea." The main purpose of the new *Princes* rested with the eight Landing Craft Assault (LCAs). In the Pacific war the Americans had been learning, sometimes the hard way, as they moved from island to island against Japanese forces who were well dug in, the art of amphibious warfare. They were developing not just landing ships of all types, and landing craft, also of many types, but the methods and tactics of amphibious operations. Getting the men to be landed near to the beaches that they were to assault was one thing. Getting them on to the beach, at the right place, at the right time, as safely and efficiently as possible was a complex business of training and logistics. It required the utmost in coordination among the naval, air and ground forces.

In 1942 Canada had experienced the price of failure when it had stormed the beaches at Dieppe, only to be repulsed with heavy losses. Of the 3716 men of Canadian regiments who were embarked for Dieppe, 2906 were either killed, missing or taken prisoner. According to the two-volume history of Canadian Naval Combined Operations "Dieppe was the first time Canadian Flotillas of the Royal Navy's Combined Operations Forces were in action against the enemy." Great Britain had also learned the hard way that landing soldiers against strongly held positions could lead to disaster. Gallipoli was one war and 38 years away, and equipment and training for amphibious warfare had not been a priority in the intervening years. The Royal Navy between the two World Wars remained essentially a big ship navy, but since 1939 their

Commandos were learning quickly the art of assault.

When the two ships sailed from New York *Prince Henry* had a few Canadian passengers while *Prince David* took on board over 400 American soldiers. Stoker Howard Eames years later recalled the Americans as "men who seemed to spend their time playing cards and dice." *Henry* also carried a number of schoolboys from Bermuda. They had been among the evacuees from Britain in 1940/41 who could now return to their families. Bill Welsh was the Yeoman of Signals in *David* so spent much time on the bridge. He noted that there were just two or three competent watch keepers among the officers. This resulted in Doug Kelly reporting to the Convoy Commodore on arrival in the UK to explain his ship's poor station keeping during the crossing. Both ships arrived without incident in the anchorage off Greenock in the river Clyde, *David* on the 28th January, 1944 and *Henry* a few days later.

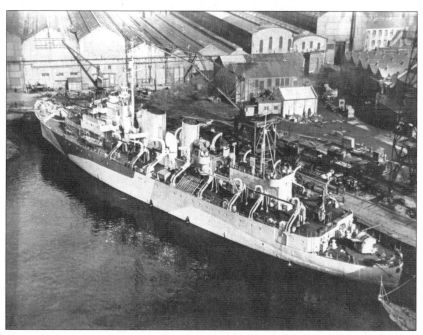

Prince David fitting out at John Brown's, Clydebank From the Ken Macpherson collection

Before the two ships could begin a period of intensive training it was necessary to complete their conversion and fitting out ready to receive the complement of LCAs. This required about two month's work performed in Clydebank by the John Brown Company. While that was being accomplished the men of the two ships either enjoyed some leave or went to various courses at Royal Navy training establishments. The improvements on board included new Oerlikons and radars and miscellaneous communications and signaling items that would be needed during the landings. When all was finished the two ships went south to the Isle of Wight.

Combined Ops sailors of Prince David Courtesy Naval and Military Museum, Calgary

At the Isle of Wight they met and loaded their contingent of LCAs. Prior to 1944 some Canadian officers and sailors had been seconded and trained with the Royal Navy. Some had been Commandos. Others had learned to load and drive the often ungainly craft to a defended and protected shore. On board each of the Canadian LSI's were the crews of the LCAs, all part of the

Three Princes Armed

company of the ship in which they served. For the eight LCA's each *Prince* ship carried five officers and 55 men. The eight craft constituted a Flotilla. *Prince Henry* carried 528 Flotilla commanded by Lieutenant (later Lieutenant-Commander) Jack Davie, RCNVR. He had been a Flotilla officer during the landings in Sicily. *Prince David* had 529 Flotilla commanded by Lieutenant Robert Buckingham, RCNVR. Virtually all the sailors of the two Flotillas were Reserves. They were Combined Ops, a breed apart from "big ship" sailors. They wore the Combined Ops badge of "hook, hawk and rifle" on their uniforms. In the two-volume pot-pourri of memories and recollections that the Combined Operations sailors printed many years later the pride still shows through. Most of their officers had had experience with them, understood their differences, and handled them accordingly.

Lieutenant Commander Hendry briefing Combined Ops members Caros, Briarley, Edwards and McLaren Library and Archives Canada copy number PD 129055

The officers of the LCA Flotillas were also able to give the authorities some bad moments when they were not training or carrying out operations. Years after the war they had regular meetings where "capers" were more often discussed than the major wartime events. The jeep incident was a favorite. In Southampton the night before sailing for the Mediterranean they entertained a US army officer. After filling him with gin they traded two bottles of gin for his jeep. They hoisted the jeep on board, had CPO McInnes paint it blue and changed the American star for a Canadian maple leaf. A jeep was very handy in the Mediterranean ports for transporting personnel on duty and on leave until a Fleet message was received giving the description and serial number of a stolen jeep. To avoid big trouble, Lieutenant Gladwell took the jeep to an area where the British 8th Army was operating. He traded the pristine machine for one that had seen much hard duty in the desert. That jeep stayed with the ship until it arrived back in the UK. In London it ran a red light, survived a police chase and was buried at sea under the East India docks.

The LCAs were built of wood with steel armour for troop protection. They had a central, fore and aft, parallel bench seating area for up to 36 men. Each craft was 58 feet long with a beam of 18 feet six inches. (some sources give different measurements). They were powered by two Ford V8 engines and could maintain a fully loaded speed of 6 knots. They had a crew of four: one coxswain, two seamen and a stoker. One officer was assigned to each group of three vessels. They shipped one light machine-gun aft. Each carried a hull number, and the crews usually painted their craft with a name much as air-crews did with their aircraft. On D-Day *Henry* sailed with numbers 736, 850, 856, 925, 1021, 1033, 1371, and 1372. *David* had 985, 1059, 1137, 1139, 1150, 1151 and 1375. She also carried a LCS(M) 101. The fates of these craft will be noted later.

With the LCAs hoisted on board Malcolm Macleod described

the new appearance of the host ships. "Hove up neatly in snug davit-harness, serially aligned along each side from quarterdeck to forecastle, the little boats from now on dominated their parent-ship's exterior prospect. With flotilla shipped, a *Prince* ship's airy waist became a dingy flat into which the sun never penetrated (though spray could fly), while davits, braces, winches and reels impeded passage through these fore-and-aft tunnels."

Now the work of preparation began. It consisted of training, training and more training. When the time came to do it all in earnest there would just be one chance to get it right. So the *Prince* ships and the LCA crews learned the mechanics of loading, lowering, driving, beaching, withdrawing from a beach, and hoisting back on board. They also had to practice the business of getting their troops on board, messing them, loading them in the proper order and sequence. When the day came for action they would also need to know where they were going, when to move, and how to get there through swept mine lanes and leading fully loaded LCI(L)s in column. Val Godfrey commented on the problems when ships of various sizes and types were required to maintain equal speeds when maneuvering in company.

The training areas required the ships to be at sea in the English Channel. They found that the enemy was able to reach them, so some of the days the exercise took on the feelings of reality. The Germans had fast E-boats that could strike quickly and then dash away. E-boats had already had one successful mission when they struck and sank two LSTs loaded with American soldiers. Six hundred of the men were lost. Enemy aircraft were still bombing the south coast of England and anti-aircraft fire was occasionally a backdrop to the training.

Winnipeg born Lieutenant "Mac" Ruttan provided the Ottawa Branch of the NOAC a splendid outline of that training period in Volume 2 of Salty Dips. Mac was not in the flotillas in the *Prince* ships, but he commanded LCI(L) *302* and they all trained in the same areas and were doing the same things. He recalled one exercise when six British soldiers were lost. The LCI had run up to the beach but heavy surf was running. When the soldiers leaped from the ramp the four-foot surf came curling back and knocked them on their backs. With fully loaded back-packs they could not stand up and were drowned. It would be the LCAs from the *Princes* that would be running to the beach. The training exercises were meant to teach the crews the many dangers they would experience.

The final rehearsal was Exercise Fabius when a huge assault force sailed from the Solent, went well out to sea at night and at dawn landed the troops on the beaches west of Portsmouth. There was then some leave ashore for the men and *Prince David* hosted the local Wrens to dinner on board. Jimmy Kaufman's diary said "the Wrens were given a large bag of goodies to take back with them."

Commander Kelly reviewing plans prior to D-Day with his staff officers. Note the sleeve stripes denoting RCNR, RCNVR and RCN. Not all the officers have adopted the new "Canada" shoulder flashes. Courtesy Maritime Museum of B.C.

Three Princes Armed

Mac Ruttan also described the very secret two-day meeting of all the Commanding Officers that was held in Southampton in early June. Both Godfrey and Kelly would have attended that meeting. Mac was thoroughly impressed with the wealth of detail and planning that, unlike the Dieppe landing, preceded the moment of execution. He said the briefers described the outline of German defences, the type, range and sector of the guns. Equally impressive were the pictures taken from submarines showing the various stages of run-in that each craft in each sector would experience and pictures of the target area on which they would land. The number of actual vessels that would be underway when the attack began was beyond any thing that had ever been accomplished in the history of warfare.

Commander Kelly addressing his ship's company prior to D-Day
Library and Archives Canada PD 345

The Allied Naval Commander for the Normandy landings was Admiral Sir Bertram Ramsay, RN. Although he died shortly before the end of the Second World War his contributions to the victory have recently been noted in an article by Tony Mead in "Seafarers" the journal of King George's Fund for Sailors. For Operation Neptune the orders ran to over 1,000 pages. Mead also wrote, "Ramsay assembled 2,468 landing craft of 46 different types, 1,656 ancillary vessels, and 1,213 escort ships." There were 5,337 ships involved in Neptune, from battleships for firepower to motor launches for route marking. The landing vessels were of all types, from ships twice the *Princes'* size to landing craft.

To be able to provide each ship with an individual plan and directions and at the same time factor in the many things that might go wrong was truly impressive. By the end of D-Day 150,000 troops had been landed, and at the end of 30 days that figure had risen to 1 million, as well as 200,000 vehicles and 700,000 tons of stores. Mead quoted Ramsay, "Because it all went so smoothly it may seem to some people that it was easy and plain sailing. Nothing could be more wrong. It was excellent planning and execution."

His Majesty King George VI reviewed the fleet of invasion craft on 24 May, and on 28 May the ships were sealed, trapping a number of British soldiers who had been temporarily on board *Prince Henry* for an exercise. General Eisenhower was the Supreme Commander and it fell to him to make the final decision as to when the attack would begin. The window of opportunity lay primarily with the dates of high tide. A high tide was necessary so that the landing craft could clear obstacles and run as far up the beach as possible. That period was 5 to 7 June after which they would have to wait for the next tidal period in late June, such a delay would have been disastrous given the massive logistics of assembling the ships and troops. The story of Eisenhower and his meteorologists is well documented. In the event, the weather was far from perfect but the decision to go was proven to be a correct one.

An LCI approaching Prince David Courtesy Naval and Military Museum, Calgary

The role of the navy was to land seven divisions of troops across a wide front in the seaward part of the operation. These seven divisions would be followed by one and one third divisions each day. In addition to the troops all the heavy equipment such as tanks and trucks, ammunition, food and petrol had to be brought ashore and delivered to the correct units. Prior to the landings the German defences were to receive a continuous overnight aircraft attack, followed by 30 minutes of daylight naval bombardment with guns of all calibers. With seven battleships, 23 cruisers, 104 destroyers plus a wide assortment of other types, the intent was to destroy as much of the defence as possible. The landings were timed to take effect just as the naval bombardment stopped.

Volume 2 of Canadian Naval Combined Operations contains an address delivered by Lloyd Williams to the Maritime Museum of Vancouver in 1995. He said that the "Canadian contribution was 110 ships and 10,000 seamen. *Prince Henry* was senior officer of Landing Ships in Force J, one of five assault Forces destined for the five sectors of the Normandy beach front. *Prince David* was to be senior ship of one of the sub-divisions of the same force." The distance from the English shore to the destination in the Baie de la Seine was 80 miles. The front on which they would land was 20 miles wide. On approach they had to maneuver in ten narrow lanes that the minesweepers had swept through the German mine fields. All of that had to be accomplished in speeds that were set and were to be maintained so that the immense ballet of movements would not be interrupted. Other specialized units were to destroy obstacles and mines that were placed to create havoc to any craft approaching inshore.

This is the story of the three *Prince* ships. There were two Canadian destroyers, numerous minesweepers, a couple of corvettes plus MTBs and various landing craft all either Canadian or manned by Canadians. Among the troops to be landed was the 3rd Canadian Infantry Division, followed by many other Canadian units. It is not proposed to review all of these actors. Malcolm Macleod faced the same issue as do today's writers. Operation "Overlord", the invasion of Europe, was on just too grand a scale to be reduced. Bookshelves are full of volumes covering every aspect of that fateful day 6 June 1944. We are concerned here only with the events that affected our two *Prince* ships and their two flotillas of LCAs.

On board *Prince Henry* were 332 men to be landed. The files of DHist show them as:

Canadian Scottish (BC) OC troops & Battalion Headquarters	153
Canadian Infantry Division Signals	2
Cameron Highlanders of Ottawa	5
7th Canadian Reconnaissance Regiment	2
234th Field Company, Royal Engineers	82

Refugee Transit Camp	30	
85th Field Company Royal Engineers	24	
1st Field Dressing Station	15	
8th Kings. Regiment	8	
Royal Army Provost Corps	8	
RN Bombardment Unit	3	Total 332

On board *Prince David* were the following;		
Regiment de la Chaudiere, 1 Company	126	
Queen's Own Rifles	258	
RCE, 16th Field Company	12	
RCE, 14th Field Reg't.	6	
22nd Field Ambulance	10	
Royal Marine Commandos	28	
Royal Army Provost Corps	12	
Royal Engineers	11	Total 463

(Note – other sources have different numbers. We choose to accept those of DHist)

Regiment da la Chaudieré in a practice load May 1944 Library and Archives Canada RCN photo A706

There must have been a master plan that dictated the composition of those troops assigned to the *Prince* ships. It was an interesting and complicated mix of Canadians and British troops to ensure that if a ship were lost no whole units would be lost. Lloyd Williams said "*Price Henry's* craft were a part of one of the flights which were to land the assault units of 7 Brigade of the Third Canadian Division on Mike Red, a mile east of Courseulles. The flights which included *Prince David's* craft were to land troops of 8 Brigade on Nan White, a mile and a half farther west." The Curator of the Queen's Own Regiment advised that the majority of the Regiment landed from the SS *Monoway* in landing serials J30 and J32.

Both the *Prince* ships led a column of the larger Landing Craft Infantry. *Henry* had nine and *David* had five. The two *Prince* ships were not meant to get too close to the beach. They followed Channels 7 and 8 until they reached their positions seven miles off shore. Lloyd Williams described the next actions as follows. "Times of arrival and deployment from the two channels had varied by only a few minutes and by 05.35 the vessels were swinging at anchor in the eerie half-dawn light, each an exact 300 yards from the next. First to be lowered into the water from *Prince David* were the two Royal Navy craft which she had carried in addition to her own. At 17 minutes after six, one of the craft, loaded with Royal Marines, went down the ship's side and set off for Nan beach where it was to provide supporting small arms fire. The second craft went in 20 minutes later, also carrying Royal Marines who were to work waist deep in the water off shore, clearing mines and obstacles ahead of the assault craft.

Then it was the turn of the Canadians. The LCAs were lowered to deck level. The soldiers emerged group by group from the troop decks and climbed quietly into their places. The two Canadian Flotillas moved to join the swarm of other landing ships assembling into beach flights, three flotillas to a flight. The LCAs would be a little over an hour in making the trip from the assault anchorage

Officers and Coxswains of Prince Henry's LCAs Courtesy Naval and Military Museum, Calgary

to the beaches." For the soldiers, making their first landing against unknown defences, this must have been one of the longest hours in their young lives. They were led in to the beaches by Motor Gun Boats which released them 4,000 yards off shore for the 15 minute run remaining. For some of them they did so without serious defensive fire.

As stated earlier it is not proposed to attempt to describe the complete run-in to the beaches or the brave, frightening, sometimes chaotic experiences that met each craft and the hundreds of LCIs that were meeting their individual fate. Malcolm Macleod collected many recollections from those on board the landing craft and some of them are reproduced here.

The following is a summary of the events covering the eight LCAs that *Prince Henry* carried as 528 Flotilla. They were sent on

their way with the best wishes of all on board including the Band of the Canadian Scottish Regiment who played them over the side into their craft.

A casualty being hoisted on board Prince David Courtesy Naval and Military Museum, Calgary

LCA *1372* – This craft took some casualties in 10 Platoon of the Canadian Scottish when a mortar bomb struck as they were disembarking. They lost one man, and several others were wounded. Able Seaman Tennant of Hamilton, Ontario, one of the crew, was also wounded. For his complete dedication to his duties and the passengers he was later awarded the Distinguished Service Medal. The LCA got away from the beach with just minor damage to her bottom. The craft then was busy running errands and help-ing other craft, alternatively grounding on the beach, and getting off, as tides rose and fell. Twice on 6 June it had to be bulldozed off into the water. It secured alongside a ship at anchor for the night, and soon after getting underway again at 0700 on the 7th was squashed between two LCTs coming in to the beach. The craft sank in one fathom, almost before the several day's ration of rum could be saved. The crew spent two more nights sleeping in LCA *1175* until they were ferried back to their parent ship. Macleod sates that the craft was destroyed by a giant bulldozer that ran over it in the surf. "The Blue Water Navy" insists that all *Henry's* craft were hoisted back on board except for LCA *1021*. The difference in these accounts is probably related to the "fog of battle."

LCA *1021* – This craft landed her troops onto their beach but was rammed by a tank that was disembarking from a British LST. The LCA caught fire and eventually sank but not before the coxswain risked his life to put out the fire. For his actions Leading Seaman D. Townson of Edmonton, Alberta, was later awarded a Mention in Dispatches. Townson was wounded, as was Leading Stoker Bielowas who was taken to another vessel for care. The remaining three from the crew got back to *Prince Henry* in one of the many vessels milling about.

LCA *1033* – The major problem for this craft was getting all its cargo of Royal Engineers to disembark. With the craft under fire the soldiers were reluctant to leave the shelter of the LCA. They finally did after some very strong words from one of the crew. The LCA then returned to *Prince Henry*. All this took place while machine gun bullets were striking the hull of the vessel. This LCA survived Neptune, Dragoon and the landings in Greece. Throughout it had been the second home to Sub-Lieutenant Flynn. He re-discovered it at the Sea Cadet camp at Comox, B.C, in 1959 and tried to purchase it from DND. Sadly it had already been sold to a private firm.

LCA *856* – This craft was commanded by Sub-Lieutenant Flynn, RCNVR, the C.O. of the Group. This was the craft in which Lieutenant Davie, the Flotilla leader was carried. His craft struck an obstacle while grounding. They took on board a wounded Corporal from the Royal Winnipeg Rifles, but their hull was holed and as they pushed off to return to *Prince Henry* they started to take water.

LCA *850, LCA 925 & LCA 1371* – these three had successfully landed their troops and were returning to *Prince Henry* when they met LCA *856* struggling to stay afloat. Davie sent LCA *850* with the wounded Corporal now on board to receive medical treatment at a Royal Navy ship. He then directed the other two to tow him by securing one to each side. Some of their crew members went on board LCA 856 to assist with the bailing. Even though the seas were quite choppy and they could only make two knots, the small group all arrived at *Prince Henry* and were hoisted safely on board. Many years after the war a then Lieutenant of the Chaudieres wrote to one of he authors stating that his craft landed on a pristine, unopposed beach a bit to the east of the planned landing area. It is difficult to reconcile an unopposed landing with all the actions on all sides of the Chaudiere beach. Perhaps the air and naval bombardments had destroyed all effective German reaction.

LCA 736 – When this craft dropped its ramp it landed on a mine that fortunately did not explode. The troops went ashore as gingerly as their weight and equipment would allow. Once clear of passengers the crew eased the craft gently on one engine until they were clear and able to return to their ship.

Prince David's craft of 529 Flotilla under Lieutenant Buckingham were not all so fortunate as were *Henry*'s.

LCS(M) *101*. One of *Prince David's* two British-manned craft fared badly at the beginning. As it was being lowered at 0620, the forward fall jammed. Macleod said "The boat swung, crazily askew, over the ugly, choppy sea, while the crew hung on. When freed, the craft smashed hard against *Prince David*'s side." The LCS did get away, engaged the targets that her Royal Marines had been given, rescued some soldiers in another LCA that was not under control, and then hit a mine and sank. Her crew and troops all made it back to the UK eventually, with just some wounds.

LCA 985. With the other Royal Marine group this craft was not so fortunate. Nothing is known of its fate except that it probably did not even make it to the area where it was to destroy the beach obstacles. The obstacles were still in place when the assault vessels reached them. Macleod reported that all those on board

985 were lost. However with the passage of time that record has been corrected by "The Blue Water Navy." That book states "The fate of her crew was unknown on board *Prince Henry* for over a week, until word reached the ship that they had managed to make their way back to England."

LCA 1150. Lieutenant Robert Buckingham, RCNVR, after steering his craft through rows of mines met a lot of enemy mortar fire as they hit the beach. They also found that the swell was making it difficult to maintain position. The tide had risen somewhat due to a delay in the schedule and many of the now hidden rocks and obstacles made it difficult to get as close inshore as they had planned. As they were in the process of landing the troops the side of the craft was struck by either a mine or a mortar shell. Buckingham in his report was not sure. Two of the soldiers were killed. LCA *1150* did not make it back to *Prince David*.

LCA 1059. The craft under Lieutenant McBeath, RCNVR, also had severe hull damage, most likely from a mine which blew in the port side. The explosion killed two of the troops. The craft broached and filled with water. The crew abandoned it.

LCA 1137. Leading Seaman La Vergne, RCN landed all his troops without any casualties but his craft suffered a large explosion from two mines that left it disabled. Another craft that did not make it back.

LCA 1138. Lieutenant Beveridge RCNVR, was able to get all his troops landed and was attempting to clear the beach when his craft had the bottom blown out. Beveridge suffered some wounds and was thrown into the water. He was saved by his coxswain, Able Seaman Cole. The craft was unable to proceed back to *Henry* and was abandoned.

LCA 1151, Lieutenant Graham RCNVR, after unloading the troops, took on board all the crews from the disabled craft on board and was attempting to ferry them back to the anchorage when the LCA was put out of action by an underwater explosion.

The stranded LCA crews eventually made it back to their ships in one of the many other landing craft milling about. The craft was earlier saved by its coxswain Leading Seaman Walker who jumped into the water and pushed aside a mine that his craft was close to striking.

The only craft from *Prince David* to survive D-Day was LCA *1375*, Lieutenant Allin RCNVR. His first task was to go to HMS *Waveney* and ferry the Headquarters group of 8th Canadian Infantry Brigade ashore. The Brigadier and his staff were so anxious to get ashore that the LCA found that they had already departed. Taking the initiative, Lieutenant Allin began acting in whatever useful role he could perform. He helped stranded personnel and continued to act as a ferry until he returned to *Prince David*, the sole survivor of the eight original craft.

Juno Beach was the landing site for all the Canadians involved in D-Day (except for those of the 1st Canadian Parachute Battalion, part of the British 3rd Para Brigade dropped on the Normandy flank). At the close of 6 June, 1,074 of the Army who participated were casualties. Of those 469 were killed. It was later learned that the Landing Craft were approaching an area in which the Germans had 11 batteries of 155mm guns, 9 batteries of 75m guns plus machine gun nests, pillboxes and mortar sites. That only seven naval personnel of the two *Prince* ships were wounded is an amazing statistic. Many of the naval participants had been well trained and had served with Royal Navy Combined Operations units so they were by and large an experienced group.

ERA Jimmy Kaufman summed up the day's rumour in his diary, "The news somehow stated that *David* was lost. The WRENs on the Isle of Wight were in shock as well as some of the people in Canada. We lost all the landing craft so for the wounded we raised the stretchers with ropes pulling hand over hand until they reached the deck. The wounded men who were still conscious opened their eyes and then closed them again knowing they were safe."

After a day that was unique in the history of warfare, a day of heroics, terror, excitement, explosions and death and destruction, it is not surprising that medals were issued. Some were of a high order, such as the Distinguished Service Medals to Leading Seaman Murray Walker of LCA *1151* and Able Seaman D. Tennant of LCA *1372*. The Distinguished Service Cross was awarded to Lieutenant Jack Davie. Others like Lieutenant Allin, Able Seaman James Cole, Stoker Petty Officer Bernard Earthy, Leading Signalman Frank Evans and Able Seaman Edwin McAuley were awarded a Mention in Dispatches. The captains of both the *Prince* ships were also awarded a Mention as were Surgeon Lieutenants J.A. Beggs RCNVR and P.G. Schwager RCNVR for their treatment of casualties. There were others who deserved and were awarded honours. There were far more who just did their duty, were wounded, terrified and at the end of the day were anonymous to historians. The formal description of the award of a Mention was phrased in the usual naval understatement, "For good service in the invasion of Normandy." Good service indeed!

Commander Kelly kept a record of his ship's movements during his period in command of *David*. His entry for 6 June concludes, "*Only one of our own men was wounded. All our Combined Operations men returned on board from an LST in the afternoon. Meanwhile we had taken aboard wounded and dead British Commandos from several LCTs. We returned at full speed to Southampton to discharge casualties to RAMC who were waiting for us with Medical Officers and ambulances.*"

Paymaster Lieutenant Jack Goodchild was in *Prince David*. Many years later he told one of the authors that his ship was not given orders for the day after D-Day so for relaxation baseball teams were landed at Cowes. One of the LCA officers who had spent the previous day landing troops at Juno Beach was accosted by one of the locals for playing baseball while "men were dying on the beach."

Doug Kelly continued with an entry for the 7th June which covered the type of activity that his ship carried out until the 14th. *"Anchorage at Cowes, Isle of Wight. We made several crossings to the French coast with reinforcements of British and Canadian troops."* For both the Canadian LSIs the period from 7 June until 14 July was one of underemployment. The men were anxious to be a fully employed part of the action but the ships were built to carry personnel and the Allies were finding that casualties were much less than had been feared and allowed for. So the troops who had landed on D-Day and the new units that were being landed had a greater need for tanks, trucks, ammunition, food and fuel than spaces for the casualties. Even the expected losses of the LCIs in the J-1 force led by *Henry* were not met. All ten returned to Cowes at the close

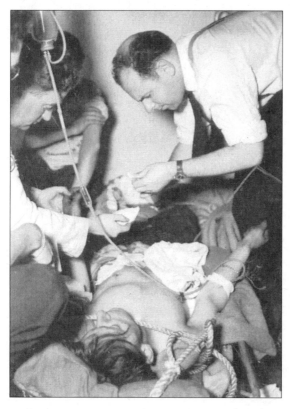

Surgeon Lieutenant J.A. Beggs treating a casualty on board Prince David Courtesy Naval and Military Museum, Calgary

of the 6 June landings. In fact there was insufficient dock space for the *Princes* as the planners had expected much more serious ship casualties than occurred.

Both *Prince* ships received replacements for the craft that they had lost, but until they sailed on 14 July for Barry, Wales they were usefully employed on very few days. Macleod said that *Henry* made five trips to France and *David* made three.

The area was not without continued danger. German V-1 flying bombs passed over their anchorage. A Royal Navy trawler was torpedoed within sight of them and a large supply vessel in the same convoy in which they were traveling was mined. Traffic across the channel was thick with ships of all types and they had to keep to the swept lanes, so navigation and attention on the bridge called for high standards. Captain Godfrey blamed the mine disaster on a slow convoy proceeding in the wrong direction in a channel that forced his convoy out of the swept channel.

After both of the *Prince* ships were given some dockyard attention, *David* in Barry, Wales and *Henry* in Southampton, they sailed on 24 July 1944 for the Mediterranean and a new chapter to their histories. They were to see much of their new operational area. Before they departed for home they were to have business in Gibraltar, Corsica, France, Italy, Albania, Greece, Malta, Tunisia and Egypt.

CHAPTER SIX

Operation Dragoon and the Mediterranean

We are as near to heaven by sea as by land!
Sir Humphrey Gilbert
Hakluyt's third Volume of the Voyages of the English Nation.

ALTHOUGH THE ALLIES HAD BY MID 1944 cleared the German army out of North Africa and were slogging up Italy against fierce German resistance, they were divided concerning the question of invading Southern France. "Monty", Nigel Hamilton's brilliant 3 Volume biography of General Bernard Montgomery, shows the separation between the British desire to keep all the armies in North-West Europe and the American belief that an invasion of southern France would be the best strategy. The American influence dominated in view of the far greater number of troops that they deployed in the battle raging in France as compared to Great Britain. As a result, Operation Dragoon, the invasion of southern France, was approved. It was known as Operation Anvil by the Americans.

With many of the landing ships no longer needed at the Normandy landings, the two *Prince* ships and their LCAs were ordered to the Mediterranean and arrived in Naples on 31 July. In early August they exercised off Agropali near Salerno and by

12 August they were in the Bay of Propriano practicing with these new assault craft. For this operation they would load their troops into rubber boats. American PT boats as well as each ship's LCAs would tow them near to the shore where they would be paddled the rest of the way. These were to be night landings, unlike the early dawn experience off Normandy. On 14 August they sailed for France. Each of the ships carried about 250 troops.

The main thrust of the amphibious assault involved three divisions of the US 7th Army and was to be centered on the French Riviera. The *Prince* ships were loaded with Commandos, some of them Canadians from the 1st Special Service Force sometimes called "Devil's Brigade." The objective for *Prince Henry* was to capture two offshore islands. For *Prince David*, her French Commandos were meant to put some mainland defences out of operation. Each of the *LSIs* carried two Landing Craft Mechanized in addition to six *LCAs*. One of the LCA officers, Lieutenant Graham, recalled many years later that the guns on the Isle d'Hyere turned out to be wooden.

Prince Henry and Prince David storing ship at Ajaccio Library and Archives Canada

LCAs from Prince David at Corsica August 1944 Naval and Military Museum, Calgary

Prince David's LCAs in practice for Operation Dragoon Library and Archives Canada RCN photo A 679

French Commandos ready to be lowered in an LCA Library and Archives Canada
PD 566

*Commander Kelly
addressing his ship's
company prior to south of
France landings* Library and
Archives Canada PD 644

Doug Kelly's diary entry on 15 August was terse but informative. "A.M. *We were at Action Stations all night. We were twelve miles off the coast of the French Riviera. Our troops having left the ship shortly after midnight, whist waiting the return of our craft we heard "Jerry" planes overhead but it was too cloudy for him to observe us. We hear our escort in action and see a big blaze ahead of us to starboard, and discover that it was a German destroyer that had been hit by gunfire from one of our cruisers. Before sinking she burned right to the water's edge when she blew in half and sank. Our main assault forces land with very little opposition. About 0700 American PT boats come alongside bringing German prisoners aboard for treatment for bad burns and exposure. Sail for Ajaccio, Corsica. Arrive at 2200.*" (Note – the Germans had no destroyers in the Mediterranean. The American destroyer USS *Somers* sank two ships, both ex-Italian Navy, manned by Germans. They were the 650 ton corvette *Comoscio* and the smaller ship *Escaburt*. Ninety-nine Germans were rescued from the sea by the *Somers* and US Navy PT boats. Many were burned from the action that sank them. The Commanding Officer of *Somers* was commended even though he risked giving away the secrecy of the operation by opening fire.

There were a number of interesting features of Dragoon. The America Rear Admiral in command of the two *Prince* ships traveled in *Prince Henry*. On board *Prince David* were Free French Commandos, an unconventional mixture from France and her North African colonies. When Doug Kelly took some of them as reinforcements to France on 17 August he described them as "*a strange mixture of Arabs, Moroccans etc. all looking very fierce.*" A story came out of *David*'s crew that one of the Colonials, a Goum, when arraigned at the Regiment's punishment table, had an ear cut off for stealing.

The actual landings were not perfect but in spite of some setbacks they generally succeeded. *Prince David* was in company with two other Landing Ships, HMS *Princess Beatrix* and HMS *Prins*

*Moroccan Goums
boarding Prince David*
Library and Archives Canada
PD 556

Albert. The landings began just before midnight. It was not a short run in. It would take over three hours, at the same time maintaining constant speeds and distances without swamping the towed craft. Fortunately the weather was kind and the sea was calm. When the crafts were less than a mile from shore they detached the rubber boats which were intended to land where the advance party of Commandos had set up a beachhead. They missed the assigned beach but no difficulties arose from the error. One of *David's* LCAs directed later LCMs loaded with mechanized equipment to the beach where the troops had landed.

Prince Henry lowered her six LCAs before midnight, all towing rubber boats. The objective was the island of Levant. The troops landed without meeting any serious opposition. Daylight showed that the "beach" was anything but. The rocky and slippery conditions made the landing of supplies a most difficult task which was partly solved with the assistance of some captured German

Prince David loading French Colonial troops Library and Archives Canada PD 566

soldiers. After disembarking their troops the LCA's spent the night assisting where possible, and were all back on board by 0900 without any casualties.

The LCMs of *Prince David* had some difficulty finding a suitable beach on which to land and offload their cargoes of mechanized equipment and stores. Finally at noon on the 17th August that was accomplished, while passing overhead according to Captain Kelly, *"Lots of gunfire from our battleships pounding German strong points inland."*

Prince Henry was now receiving casualties as well as prisoners. On board were her two doctors, Surgeon Lieutenant-Commander G.E. Large, RCNVR and Surgeon Lieutenant H.A. McDougall, RCNVR. When medical services could no longer cope with the numbers some patients were transferred and both *Prince* ships sailed for Ajaccio where they could disembark both the casualties and the prisoners. They both made two additional trips to the south of France, often with more of the strange soldiers of the

Three Princes Armed

French colonial world. Operation Dragoon came to an end for the Canadian ships on 24 August. Malcolm Macleod summarized it with the following. "The south of France was unique among the great amphibious operations of the Second World War in being more of an end than a beginning. Its smoothness and strength was the culminated harvest of an impressive series of Mediterranean landings stretching back to "Torch", although the strategic seeds it sowed were probably planted in the wrong garden as Churchill thought. What cannot be denied is the invasion's professionalism. Allied expertise had been emphasized in this account of the RCN participation."

Macleod notes that some mistakes and problems were experienced by the Canadians but the landings were successful in every aspect and only one landing craft of the Canadian contingent was damaged by the enemy. Doug Kelly's only complaint was the extent of briefings and complicated orders. It is significant to note that the two *Prince* ships arrived in the Mediterranean on 29 July and participated in the Dragoon landings just over two weeks later. Another factor of note is that during their lives the three *Prince* ships most often operated under the operational control of either the Royal Navy or the United States Navy. Obviously they knew their business and the respective captains easily adjusted to direction from other than their official masters in Ottawa. Both ships now returned to Italy, *Henry* to Castelamare for boiler cleaning and *David* to Taranto.

Lieutenant Commander Davie was awarded the Distinguished Service Cross for his leadership of the two Flotillas over the period of both the Neptune and Dragoon assaults. The other Flotilla commander, Lieutenant Buckingham was awarded a Distinguished Service Cross "For services in the successful invasion of the south of France."

The Mediterranean
HMCS Prince David
September 1944 To February 1945

The diary of Captain Kelly provides a personal background to the remaining Mediterranean service of his ship. He and his ship's company were not pleased with Taranto. *"Sept. 2nd Leave for Taranto, an important Italian Naval Base situated in the heel of Italy. On having leave here we find it a not very impressive place, and the people almost hostile towards us. On the 11th of Sept. we left for Brindisi, arriving there on the 12th. Only to return to Taranto. Sept. 14th Left Taranto with British Commandos, ammunition and equipment for invasion of Greek Island of Cerigo. Sept. 15th Approaching the island at dusk during a heavy swell, port LCM was lowered prematurely to deck level and the swinging motion caused the davit to collapse leaving loaded LCM dragging in the sea. LCM contained two field guns, one jeep and ammunition. Also large amount personal belongings. LCM eventually capsized and was lost. Commandos took island without opposition. Natives cheered them as they landed."*

Malcolm Macleod reported this as Operation Aplomb. He described the passage wherein *David* was protected en route by three British and one Polish destroyer, the Royal Navy escort aircraft carrier HMS *Khedive*, and six minesweepers, as she sailed through the narrow Kithera Channel. Intelligence had reported a U-boat in the vicinity, and with more than 500 soldiers on board extreme protection was taken. He noted that when LCM *185* was lost there were no casualties.

It was not at all clear whether the Germans had remained on the island. So the loss of the field gun was potentially important, as was the loss of the LCM and the load of ammunition. Macleod described the landing *"at 2128 the ship anchored a discreet half-mile offshore. The seven-craft assault wave was sent away at 2140,* while *Prince David's* guns crews closed up to give covering fire if necessary. The Flotilla Officer's LCA led the way into the narrow cleft in the rocks that forms the harbour of the fishing village of Saint Nikolo. Bren guns were mounted on the deck of the craft along either side, and the ship's Chaplain had found room behind one of them. The first two craft crept in on silent engines ahead of the others to see if the harbour was defended but they touched down unopposed at the head of the harbour, the only possible landing place. After a look around the other craft were signaled in." LCA *1432* had been damaged on the run in when it struck a submerged obstacle but that was the only casualty. That LCA was hoisted on board where repairs were made by the competent engineering department under Lieutenant (E) Austin Wright.

Between 16 September and 8 October the ship was either in Taranto or Brindisi where the davit was repaired and the men had a chance to enjoy some shore leave. There was a return to operations on the 8th when she sailed for the Greek island of Poros in company with the RN destroyer HMS *Eggesford*. In his diary Kelly noted that this escort was heard firing during the night. He does not mention an Allied Liberator aircraft that Macleod says dropped a stick of bombs that came close to *David*. On arrival at Poros the landing craft were lowered and left there with their crews while the ship returned to Taranto.

At this point in the careers of both the *Prince* ships their involvement with Greece became more intense and potentially sensitive from a political standpoint. As the Germans were withdrawing, the various factions within Greece began to fight among themselves for post-war supremacy. One of these groups was the Communist element. The actions of the Canadian ships were as ordered by the British under whose operational control they were. The British policy was to take control of Athens as soon as the Germans had departed and to install the legitimate pre-war government who were not Communists. Operation Manna was the plan by which the liberation of Athens would be conducted and *David* was a first team player. Her landing craft had been left in Greek waters when she returned to Taranto.

Macleod described the event. "*Prince David's* landing craft were preparing the way. Four days were spent undergoing artillery barrages and planning attacks on two islands. Then word was received that the Germans had withdrawn from the islands and also from the capital. At 0100 14 October No.529 Flotilla sailed to spearhead the seaborne landing at Piraeus, the port for Athens. Also in this first liberation convoy were two Royal Navy Landing Craft Tank, with the 9th Commando and 200 ranks of the Greek Sacred Brigade embarked. When one of the assault craft was sent ahead to scout Piraeus and choose the best place for beaching, the Canadians became the first Allies to enter Piraeus harbour since 1940."

When the British and Greek troops landed they were met by masses of cheering Greeks some of whom filled the harbour with all manner of boats. It was virtually a mob scene with LCA *1115* being invaded and boarded by a full load of excited Greek females.

As more of the Allied ships arrived, the harbour became filled with ships at anchor, all of whom had stores or personnel that they wanted to land. So *David's* landing craft responded to the many requests for moving stores, looking for landing spaces and ferrying personnel. They were fully occupied for the next two days.

In Taranto *Prince David* was about to also take on ferry duties but these were for some very important Greek people. Captain Kelly's diary was laconic in his description. "*Oct. 13th Take on supplies, troops and high ranking officials. Oct. 14th Greek Prime Minister and staff arrive on board. Leave for Poros to deliver P.M. and staff after four years in exile. Oct. 17th Greek P.M. addresses ship's company. Proceed cautiously to Piraeus through minefields laid by the enemy. Minesweepers were seen blowing up mines every few minutes. Port of Piraeus was really smashed up. Hundreds of natives were cheering on the jetty as we went in. The people were very happy to be liberated.*

There was a bad feeling between the two political groups. Guerillas were
parading menacingly along the streets of Piraeus and Athens."

Doug Kelly did not mention that his passenger list for this trip
consisted of no less than 384 people, including some in the so-
called "high ranking" group consisting of Georgios Papandreou
the P.M., a Greek Admiral, five Greek Ministers of State, and the
British Ambassador. The domestic arrangements on board required
numerous adjustments with members of the wardroom and messes
fitting the visitors in as well as the limited spaces permitted. The
ship's Paymaster Sub-Lieutenant hosted the Chief of the Greek
Naval Staff and the Co-Director of the bank of Greece in his cabin.
These crowded conditions would have been relieved on Tuesday
17th according to the plan for Manna. But since Tuesday was considered to be an unlucky day in Greece's history, the landing was
delayed one day.

Government officials returned to Greece by Prince David Library and Archives
Canada PD 694

The Prime Minister was finally transferred to the ancient Greek cruiser *Georgios Averoff* (built 1910) from which ship he made his ceremonial arrival in his native capital. The Greek government felt that the act of bringing home the legitimate leaders of Greece was worthy of recognition. A silver, engraved bowl on a base was later presented to *Prince David*. The bowl is now held by the Naval and Military Museum in Esquimalt. The inscription reads "The Royal Hellenic Government, To HMCS *Prince David* in Remembrance of the Journey of Liberation 18 October 1944."

At dawn on the 18th *David* recovered her flotilla of landing craft and on the 18th October sailed. On arrival in Piraeus there was a rapturous welcome afforded to the Canadian sailors by the Greeks, which included the ship's Flotilla receiving 50 bottles of champagne, one for each of its members. Jimmy Kaufman noted in his diary "We were ashore in Piraeus and Athens many times. We obtained some books from a local Gestapo Headquarters, one was Mein Kampf. We arrived 24 hours after the Germans left. There was a large keg of beer half full!!"

LCAs at Piraeus Library and Archives Canada PD 762

Three Princes Armed

Captain Kelly's comments on his ship's next destination reflected the crew's feelings. "*Sailed for Taranto. Lots of rumors as to length of time for repairs. Ship's company were feeling miserable at the prospect of a long stay here. Leave granted for a few days at Bari Rest Camp.*"

Prince David was in the dockyard for maintenance until 7 November, when she returned to Piraeus, this time to enjoy a period of leave in Athens. Doug Kelly's comments show the state in which the harbour had been left by the Germans and what the city itself was soon to become by the open conflict between the warring Greeks. "*Shore leave in Athens a very interesting and historical city. Extent of damage to the city is very light. A group of us visited the Acropolis accompanied by a Greek guide. Grand panoramic view from Parthenon. Many sunken ships could be seen lying in the harbour at Piraeus. These ships were sunk by the Germans before leaving for the purpose of blocking our entry.*"

When the leave period concluded on 20 November the ship began a period of ferrying. First there were two trips with Greek soldiers to Preveza on the north-west coast of Greece. The first group was disembarked on the 25th in rough seas. The second group of 276 was put ashore at the end of November. These soldiers were soon defeated by dissident elements and the survivors were later evacuated by *Prince Henry*.

On 1 December *David* sailed to Patras and took on board some police whose wives and domestic animals had to be left behind. Back in Piraeus on the 3 December Kelly and his ship found a different and unhealthy scene. Macleod said "A general strike had been called in the capital, and as *Prince David* came to anchor the first clash between police and civilians was occurring outside the apartment where the Prime Minister lived." Kelly's description shows how quickly things had gone downhill ashore. "*Once again we arrive at Piraeus to find Hell a poppin.*" Anti-British elements were seen sniping from the rooftops at Greek soldiers and Allied tanks which

LCAs from Prince David landing Greek troops at Syros November 1944
Library and Archives Canada PD 767

were patrolling the streets. This we could see plainly from the ship for it was all going on in the dock area. Very unhealthy, no shore leave. After considerable delay we finally board the POWs. We then take on Italian POWs to return them to Taranto. These did not appear to be the great aggressive fighter that Mussolini tried to make the rest of the world believe. Arrived Taranto 6th December and once again see the Henry and compare notes with some of the boys."

The contingent of police was landed as quietly as possible on the early morning of the 4th using the landing craft of 529 Flotilla. When *David* sailed for Taranto later that day it was to sever her long period of being mother ship for the hard working men and craft of that Flotilla.

On 8 December *David* took British Paratroopers to Piraeus. Kelly described them as a "well trained outfit." He had also taken on a cargo of ammunition that was stowed on deck as well as below.

Three Princes Armed

But his arrival near Piraeus this time was to not only find a rapidly deteriorating situation ashore, but also involved near disaster for his ship. "*Prince David proceeding to Piraeus hits mine. Mine blows a hole right through bow below water line. No casualties and we proceed to Piraeus slowly. Explosion shook the ship pretty bad, radar and Asdic gear out of order. Lots of small warships in harbour. Destroyers bombard Communist ELAS gun positions in the hills outside Piraeus. Shooting very accurate. The trouble ashore has developed into a real war now. Numerous casualties and the horrible tales of the torturing of British prisoners. An outfit of Ghurkas is reported going to town in real style. In the night the shell, rifle and mortar fire makes a strange sight. From a half a mile off shore we can see smoke from fires in Athens.*"

The sea lanes into Piraeus had been constantly swept by the minesweepers but ships were still being sunk. The mine that struck *David* had most likely drifted into the channel. It was an unlucky moment for the first of the *Prince* ships to be damaged by enemy activity in the long months of warfare. Macleod described the blast as "an underwater explosion lifted the bow of the ship some three or four feet. From the bridge a flash or spray was visible, although eyewitnesses who were on he upper deck report seeing a column of spray some 15 or 20 feet high on the port side just forward of the bridge. The shock of the explosion was sufficient to throw several men who were standing on the forward section of the upper deck off their feet." When the ship moved into Salamis Bay she anchored, and her hull was examined by a Royal Navy diver. There was some flooding in a small number of the forward compartments. There was one small hole on the starboard side and a much larger 17 by 12 foot hole on the port side.

Paymaster Lieutenant Jack Goodchild said that it was like hitting a snow bank when the mine blew. All sorts of gear fell down. One Petty Officer Painter had taken to sleeping in the paint locker that was well forward in the ship. The blast blew him out of his bed and sprayed his whole body with all colours of paint.

Engineers checking mine damage to Prince David at Tunis Library and Archives
Canada PD 794

Doug Kelly's main concern now was for the repair of his ship. After off-loading the cargo of ammunition into landing craft he was ordered to Malta and with the unprepared hole in the bow had to proceed very slowly. He arrived there on 16 December. Malta by this point in the war had been bombed to where in some areas it was no more than rubble. The ship remained there for just two days and on 17 December sailed for a repair base at Ferryville, Tunisia.

Jimmy Kaufman's diary provides a fairly accurate description of how the "lower deck" personnel took advantage of this protracted time in Dockyard hands. "We arrived at Ferryville, Tunisia for repairs. The *Prince David* was in dry-dock so this gave us some time to clean the boilers etc. The stokers carried the dirt ashore in sacks. When they returned with the sacks they had a few bottles of wine. The local Arabs waited for the crews going ashore. They would buy anything or sell you anything. Most of us sold our civvies which we had stored away. The wine was for parties. Being the Christmas season I saved up about 90 oz. of rum from my tots each day. We had a great party! One engineer officer made it to the party with a broken leg."

Back in the Adriatic, the two Flotillas of landing craft became the responsibility of *Prince Henry* for a period until that ship left the area for other duties. Often even while being struck by small arms fire, 529 Flotilla continued with the many and varied tasks involving the movement of stores and personnel, transferring artillery pieces, ferrying casualties and conducting some beach assaults. One of those assaults was described by Macleod. "A friendly radio station on the shore of Phalerun Bay was besieged by ELAS (the insurgents) and begged assistance."

The landing craft (three from *David* and one from *Henry*) embarked troops at Port Mahonnes and made passage in a strong 25 knot wind that threw up choppy seas and drove spray like hail. Even in somewhat sheltered waters, conditions were clearly marginal for such light craft that tossed about and were a prey to every gust of wind and slop of sea. They nevertheless bucked along bravely and dashed in through a terrific mad-cap surf about 1900. Two of *Prince David's* craft (*1373* and *1375*) broached to on the beach. Despite the best efforts of their crews they could not be pointed properly seaward again before high breakers rolled in, rocked them over and filled them with water. Nobody was hurt and the soldiers got off to their objective all right. But the shipwrecked sailors had to abandon their craft without salvage. They returned in LCA *1432* to *Prince Henry*. On 15 December the Flotilla Officer of 528 inspected the two craft and they were both recovered. LCA *1375* was repaired but LCA *1373* remained hanging from a davit on *Prince Henry*.

Because *Prince Henry* was now mother ship to both Flotillas, her davits could not accommodate all the landing craft. So the extra craft were left in the water and secured to quarter-booms. In the evening LCA *1346* broke loose and was swept away by the stormy seas. The following day it was found ashore, swamped and unable to be recovered due to the high surf that was running. On the 15th it was pulled off the beach, showing a hole in the stern. Two landing craft tried to tow it to *Prince Henry*. It became obvious that the tow could not be maintained without danger so the lines were cut. LCA *1346* sank in 15 fathoms alongside the mother ship. There was no loss of life.

By 21 December the original 16 landing craft of the two Flotillas was reduced by losses to 13. Over that night they joined in their last assault for 1944. It involved three battalions of troops, and the target area was the north shore of the harbour of Piraeus. Macleod describes the event, "H-hour 0300. No opposition was expected nor was it encountered initially. The object was to land the troops undetected and all craft made their approaches skillfully and quietly. The initial advantage of surprise was achieved on all beaches and was a great help to the army. Satisfaction with the work of both major and minor landing craft was expressed by General Scobie. At about 0600 sniping from the north shore at the loading jetty started and work there was unpleasant for about three hours. Slight damage was done to the craft skippered by Lieutenant G. Hendry. Later in the morning mortaring started but was inaccurate and ineffective. Craft were employed evacuating wounded and dead and some hundreds of ELAS prisoners during the remainder of the day and similarly during 23 December."

When *Prince Henry* left Piraeus, 529 Flotilla moved to a Royal Navy barracks area where they spent Christmas Eve. For the balance of 1944 they continued with whatever harbour duty was assigned to them, occasionally being fired at but also being welcomed by the civilians who viewed Canadians as liberators. Conditions were becoming much quieter by the New Year and the craft carried on this routine until 15 January when *David* came to retrieve them.

Prince David's repairs had been completed by 11 January and the ship was fumigated in Bizerta on the 12th. The ship's company was happy to leave the area described by Doug Kelly as *"not a very nice place at all. Rains nearly every day."* On 15 January they sailed for Piraeus where they found that two landing craft were missing. They then sailed to Taranto with almost 400 members of the Highland Light Infantry. On 22 January *David* was in Messina where, except for LCA *1375*, her old and somewhat battered craft were off- loaded and seven new landing craft were embarked. A trip to Augusta followed, then to Malta with some R.N. personnel, then back to Augusta for a period of leave and relaxation.

By now the planners in Ottawa and the Admiralty in London had agreed on the future for the two *Prince* ships. That decision will be described later in this chapter. Doug Kelly described the immediate result for his ship. *16 Feb. "Sailed for Gibraltar. 19 Feb. Arrived Gibraltar for onward routing home – we hope. 20 Feb. Left Gibraltar for Curacao, Dutch island off Venezuela. 1 March Arrived Curacao for oil. Had an uneventful voyage from Gib. Good weather all the way with climate getting warmer. Left for Colon, Canal Zone same evening. 3 March Arrived Colon and went through canal at 1400. At 1900 we arrived at Balboa. After taking on stores we left Canal Zone en route to our home port of Esquimalt."* Prince David arrived home on 14 March 1945 and was placed in Care and Maintenance. The remainder of her story is told in the next chapter.

The Mediterranean
HMCS Prince Henry
August 1944 To March 1945

The boiler cleaning of *Prince Henry* was completed by the middle of September. She then moved to Taranto where from time to time the two Canadian ships would meet and exchange information and experiences. Her first duties were to act as a ferry, taking damaged landing craft to Messina in Sicily where the Allies had established a repair facility. During that period in October her own 528 Flotilla was detached to make davit spaces for her loads. *Henry* also did a troop lift of New Zealanders from Bari to Ancona. In mid-October one somewhat abortive attempt to assist British forces landing on the Albanian coast resulted in temporarily loaning four of her *LCAs*. Back in Taranto 528 Flotilla rejoined her. Greece then became her center of operations.

Canadian naval and historical interest has long centered on the Battle of the Atlantic, and that battle properly belongs in the forefront. Some Canadians manned British Motor Gun Boats and Motor Torpedo Boats in the Mediterranean. Some of the Canadian corvettes took North African convoys past Gibraltar and were responsible for the sinking of two Italian submarines. But the operations of the two *Prince* ships never received much "press" or review during or after the war. Their role in Grecian waters had as much to do with British foreign policy as it did with winning the war. The Germans were moving out of Greece by the fall of 1944, so the protagonists were more often Greeks in opposition to each other than the traditional German enemy. The two *Prince* ships now took all their direction from whatever British authority was in command. This was not a new situation. For almost all of their operational activity during the war the three *Prince* ships were under either Royal Navy or United States Navy control rather than their national masters in Ottawa.

Prince Henry's first task as part of Operation Manna was to take 408 army troops for a landing at Piraeus. 528 Flotilla had no trouble with getting the army on shore, and then began additional duties of ferrying personnel and stores. Where possible the crews joined in the celebrations that expressed the joy of the Greeks at their liberation. *Henry* also made two more troop movements from Taranto on 24 October and 2 November.

Captain Val Godfrey, C.O. of Prince Henry Library and Archives Canada PD 511

At the beginning of November *Henry* was directed to support Operation Kelso. The intention was to place a strong British force in Salonika, in the north-west corner of the Aegean, to counteract the growing unrest in that district. On 7 November *Henry* was part of a large fleet of ships that delivered three to four thousand troops and supplies to the landing area. Macleod provides a description of the landings. "Next morning because of the danger of mines to the larger ships and because more troops were rather urgently needed ashore, it was decided to unload the convoy by landing craft without moving the larger ships into Salonika Bay. This meant that landing craft had to make trips 15 to 18 miles in open waters along swept channels which, in the approaches to the harbour, narrowed down to five cables (1,000 yards) in width. *Prince Henry's* craft were in the first flight and they left their ship at 0600. No craft in the assault flight came to grief on the many mines which certainly remained in the harbour and for the troops as well as the landing craft it was the most innocuous D-day on record."

Prince Henry at Taranto, Italy The Ken Macpherson collection

With her Flotilla employed *Henry* remained at anchor for the next two weeks. On the 20th she sailed to Piraeus and on the 22nd she arrived in Taranto to again begin the ferrying of landing craft to Messina. During the ferrying she left 528 Flotilla in Taranto. It is unfortunate that the crew in *Henry*, unlike *David*, did not leave a diary so that the two ship's company's feelings for Taranto might have been compared.

Prince Henry returned to Piraeus with a contingent of the Essex

Regiment on 7 December. While at anchor *Henry* learned that in war, danger does not always come from one's enemy. The corvette HMS *La Malouine* was firing her four-inch gun at targets in Piraeus. Some of the shells began landing much too close to *Henry* who quickly found a safer anchorage. The troops were landed on 9 December. As conditions deteriorated ashore in Piraeus so did dangers grow for the offshore ships. *Henry* was struck by a rifle bullet on 11 December and even her landing craft were fired at by small arms, possibly even from Allied ships.

Earlier the assault on the radio station at Phalerun Bay was described. *Prince Henry's* contribution was just one landing craft. Later LCA 1396 from *Henry*, under Lieutenant J.A. Flynn, RCNVR attempted to join the four assault craft. He had on board a small army group with an Artillery Forward Observation Officer. Sea conditions were extreme and he fell well behind his schedule, so he secured alongside HMS La *Malouine*. The decision was taken to abort the mission and the LCA was secured aft to a wire rope. Before dawn Flynn was called by the duty watch because his craft was bouncing and placing a strain on the wire. As he arrived on deck the wire snapped, the craft capsized and sank. Flynn and his crew were recovered by the Flotilla Officer of the mother ship on the morning of 15 December. This was the same period when *David* had lost two of her craft, all of these due more to weather than enemy action. On 21 December the firing on shore again intensified and more bullets struck *Prince Henry*. That night 528 Flotilla participated in the assault on the north shore of Piraeus which has been earlier described.

At midnight on 23 December *Henry* was ordered to proceed with dispatch to Preveza, on the west coast, where the Greek army was in trouble. Christmas day found *Henry* anchoring off Preveza. The Communists of ELAS were closing in on the area and evacuation of civilians as well as military was begun. All that day the landing craft shuttled back and forth from the town jetty to the ship, each load consisting of seasick women and children, goats, chickens, sheep and dogs. Fortunately some of *Henry*'s ship's company spoke enough Greek to shout orders, but it was a very non-naval conglomeration of humans and beasts that milled about on the deck. By late evening at least 1,100 people had been taken on board and when daylight came on 26 December *Henry* sailed north to Corfu. Feeding this many was accomplished by the galley creating enough soup and bully beef sandwiches, but cultural differences required *Henry*'s officers and men to ensure that the Greek men did not take precedence over the children and nursing mothers and pregnant passengers. The ship arrived at Corfu by mid-afternoon without any of the pregnancies advancing the numbers of passengers on board.

Prince Henry loading Greek soldiers Library and Archives Canada Copy # C008222464 PH 508

On 27 December *Prince Henry* made a second trip to Preveza. She took on board the remaining civilians and then began taking the Greek soldiers who had been defeated by the Communists. Having learned from the first trip that confusion would result unless order was maintained, the ship landed a party of sailors under Lieutenant-Commander John Bracken, RCNVR. When they sailed at midnight there were about 1,500 evacuees on board including over 1,300 Greek soldiers. Many of the latter believed that they would get cabin accommodations. They were quickly disabused of such thoughts. Private (and locked) accommodation was provided to three German deserters who were identified among the soldiers. *Henry* arrived at Corfu the next morning and disembarked this, the largest load of people carried to date by any of the LSIs.

With Preveza about to fall to the ELAS forces it was necessary for *Henry* to make a third and last trip to that town on 29 December, this time to take the remaining soldiers and whoever else needed to escape. It was a strange mixture of over 800 Greek soldiers, over 500 Italian prisoners of war, a few civilians and, strangest of all, 50 Russians, apparently civilians. *Henry* sailed in the late afternoon and Preveza fell to ELAS the next morning. All the Greeks were taken to Corfu on 30 December. The Italian POWs were taken to Taranto along with the Russians and disembarked on the last day of 1944.

Prince Henry had played a major role in this operation which took, all together, over 10,700 persons to safety. The ship was constantly overloaded, placing great strains on her ship's company who had to accommodate, feed, provide sanitary facilities and then clean up the mess after they departed. This had to be accomplished at the same time as they ensured the safety of the ship that was either loading or sailing for 24 hours each day. Most of the sailing was done in the night hours in waters that were new to those on watch who may have found it difficult to get the kind of sleep that is required for safe navigation and pilotage. Captain Val Godfrey, like most good captains, would not have been far from his bridge for all these days, and it is a tribute to him and his officers and men that the three trips were executed safely and expeditiously. The relief of Preveza may have been a "backwater" in the broad spectrum of the war at that stage but to the thousands of Greeks who were saved, it was one of the more important events of the war.

The New Year began with an immediate operation. The ship took on board a contingent of New Zealand soldiers and sailed on 2 January. These 300 plus men were disembarked at Alexandria, Egypt on 5 January. The dockyard at Alexandria was one of the principal facilities of the Royal Navy and for the following six weeks the ship was given a boiler cleaning and general repair and maintenance, which, given the recent activities, must have been very much overdue. Her ship's company enjoyed some very much needed leave, in a safer haven.

With no further requirement for Landing Ships for assault operations in the Mediterranean or Europe, the next direction for the two Canadian ships was significant, as *Henry* was completing her refit. The argument in Ottawa had already been very much settled which removed the possibility of sailing through the Suez Canal to South-East Asian waters. That argument is clearly and cogently discussed in "A Blue Water Navy" (pages 516 to 519). The Prime Minister, Mackenzie King, did not want Canadian forces to be part of any British attempts to liberate former colonies in that area. Canadian participation in the Pacific war was to be limited to 13,000 naval personnel afloat, and all to be in the northern hemisphere. The British had originally planned that both *Prince Henry* and *Prince David* would participate in Operation Dracula, an assault on Rangoon, Burma. As a result of King's decision, the only way that the two ships would be used for Dracula required them to be turned over to Great Britain and manned by the Royal Navy. The Admiralty agreed to that proposition.

The dockyard period for *Prince Henry* was finished by mid

February and she sailed for Messina. At Taranto on 24 February she embarked 280 men of the Royal Artillery and took them to Piraeus where they disembarked on 26 February. On 27 February a similar number of gunners were taken to Salonika where they were exchanged for some of the Essex Regiment who were taken to Volos on the Greek mainland. At Volos *Henry* loaded about 200 Greek civilians who had the misfortune to have anti-Communist sympathies and they were taken to Piraeus, arriving on 4 March.

When *Henry* left Piraeus for the last time on 5 March it was with a serious problem in her starboard engine. After delivering her passengers at Taranto, she sailed to Malta where emergency repairs were made which allowed a maximum speed of just 15 knots. She departed Malta on 15 March and arrived at Gibraltar on 18 March. At Gibraltar she embarked her last load of passengers, some 270 people who needed a "lift" home. It was fortunate that these ships were built as liners and designed with galleys that could feed large numbers. It is not known whether any of the support staff of Cooks and Supply Assistants on board were ever recommended for recognition. They certainly deserved something. They did not know from one day to the next who, or how many, mouths they would be required to feed. And there must have been some religious or dietary problems.

Human passengers were not the only feeding requirements on board the two *Prince* ships. Over a period of time they had collected an interesting array of live-in pets. The war correspondent Wallace Rayburn reported in the Standard Magazine of 2 December 1944. *Prince David* had a pair of pigeons which had been frightened by gunfire during the invasion of Southern France and had flown aboard. They decided to remain. *Prince Henry* by comparison ran a regular zoo. It consisted of three black cats, a canary, a cocker spaniel and a pekinese. One of the cats slept each night in a small hammock specially made for it.

Macleod described her last few days as a Canadian warship

"*Prince Henry* reached England on 27 March. She spoke in passing by signals to an old friend, HMS *Ulster Monarch* (another Landing Ship) whom she had led to the beaches of Normandy, as she came into the Thames through Sheerness boom at 1530. Commander-in-Chief Nore was not happy to see her. His message to Admiralty complained that he had only been told to expect her on the 26th, and not informed she had over 330 passengers including invalids, until London telephoned at noon on the day she arrived. Onward transportation for the home-coming servicemen could not be laid on in an instant, so he had *Prince Henry* disembark her people into already overcrowded Chatham barracks. On 29 March she got underway for the last time as an RCN warship making a short passage up the historic Thames to secure to East India Docks."

One more ceremony was performed before the majority of her ship's company were drafted ashore for return home. The Canadian High Commissioner, Vincent Massey, inspected the ship's company at "Divisions" on 5 April. On 15 April the ship was paid off from the RCN and commissioned by the Royal Navy under Lieutenant-Commander AFC Gray, RNR. *Prince Henry* was the first of the *Prince* ships to end her wartime career. The post-war careers of all three ships follow in later chapters.

"*Elephant's Graveyard*" *Prince David and Prince Robert awaiting disposal by War Assets Commission, Lynn Creek, Vancouver, 1946.*
Image E-01804 courtesy of Royal B.C. Museum, B.C. Archives

CHAPTER SEVEN

Prince Henry And The Quiet Life

To entertain this lag-end of my life with quiet hours
Shakespeare, "Henry IV", Part 1, Act 5 (1579)

AFTER HER BUSY CAREER IN THE MEDITERRANEAN Prince Henry and the other two sister ships became the subject of discussions between the Admiralty and the Canadian Navy. The former was already committed to establishing a British Pacific Fleet (the BPF) for the post-German-war attacks on Japan. The Americans would no doubt continue to provide by far the larger forces there, and tended to be suspicious of British future intentions in regard to their old colonies and protectorates in the Far East.

On 18 November 1944, the Admiralty suggested that if Canada was not prepared to man the three *Princes* for Pacific operations in the South-East Asia area, they could be transferred to the Royal Navy who would take them over. NSHQ eventually decided to retain two ships for that potential role. *Prince Robert* was becoming available since the German air threat in the European areas had much diminished and she would be useful to the BPF as AA protection for their aircraft carriers. *Prince David* was being employed as simply a troop and refugee transport. As the Greek situation was stabilizing slowly, she would seem to be available by the end of 1944.

But a third ship, if this Pacific conflict manning requirement developed, was more than the Canadian Navy was prepared to meet. Those Regular Force career officers in Naval Headquarters were, as always, much more interested in the RCN acquiring and manning destroyers, preferably the large Tribals, and the cruisers they had arranged to acquire from the RN – true "warships", not converted passenger vessels - so it was agreed that *Henry* would be turned over to the RN as the Admiralty had suggested.

She sailed for England via Gibraltar in March 1945, and at London's East India Docks at noon on 15 April she was paid off from Canadian service, her crew were drafted ashore for other duties, and replaced by RN officers and men. She was technically on loan to the RN at this stage, to be returned to the RCN at some later date to be decided. Re-commissioned in May as HMS *Prince Henry* she sailed for Wilhelmshaven on the German Baltic coast as an accommodation and headquarters ship for Allied forces occupying that large naval port. Due to the massive bombing destruction there in the latter days of the war there were few buildings that were useable in the city. She was not the first *Prince Henry* in RN service, as there had been a sailing 5th Rate warship of that name in 1747, named for a son of George III.

Toward the end of 1945 she returned to England and lay at a mooring at Falmouth on the south Cornish coast, looking rather desolate and unkempt, while the British decided if they had further employment for her. Being still the actual property of the Canadian Navy, they confirmed that they had no further need of her and in late 1946 the ship was sold for $500,000 by Canada's War Assets Corporation to the British Ministry of Transport. In dockyard hands she was fitted out for troop carrying at Harland and Wolff's at Southampton. She was repainted with a black hull and funnels and light grey superstructure (these colours were changed several times during her trooping career), renamed His Majesty's Transport (HMT) *Empire Parkeston*, and placed under the management of the venerable General Steam Navigation Company for her operation. The sobriquet *Empire* was widely used for British ships built or taken over by the Government during the war. She was to continue to serve the Forces, as on 4 April 1947 she was put to trooping between Parkeston Quay at Harwich on the Essex coast at the mouth of the Rover Stour and the Fruit Wharf at Hoek van Holland - the Hook of Holland. The *Parkeston* was then the largest trooper operating out of that port. In her new employment the eight LCAs were replaced by 10 conventional lifeboats, her appearance otherwise little changed except for the removal of all armament. In a curious reconnection with these ships' histories, it was on this same route between the UK and Holland that their originator, Henry Thornton, had gained his first shipping experience with British Great Eastern Railway's ferry connections.

Three ships were to be employed on this run, after it had been cleared of mines, replacing other ships that had been on the Harwich – Hook route since 30 July 1945 but were now required in their pre-war jobs. The service outward from Britain handled returning ex-prisoners-of-war to Germany and other displaced persons to Europe, and taking troops over and back for the B.A.O.R. – the British Army of the Rhine. The returning prisoners were all gone by the latter part of 1947, but moving the Army of occupation continued for another 40 years. Most materiel shipping requirements went into the Continent via the River Scheldt and Antwerp, and as harbors were repaired and mines the retreating Germans had liberally sown were removed, other ports were used such as Calais. But the trooping service to the Hook was the primary one for military passengers.

The three ships involved were the *Empire Parkeston*, the seized ex-German motor ship *Linz*, now *Empire Wansbeck* (slightly smaller, with about half the crew and yet carrying more troops, 1,020), and the elderly British ex-LNER ferry and trooper *Vienna*. For one year another ship the *Biarritz* joined them, but was soon scrapped. Each

Empire Parkeston ex-Prince Henry   Author's collection

ship was managed by a different shipping company on behalf of the government, despite their almost identical duties, and those companies provided crew, fuel, stores, repairs and maintenance. This was all overseen by the Sea Transport Service to meet the Forces' personnel movement requirements, with representatives at all ports, including Harwich and the Hook. It was a system that is reported to have worked quite well. Up to 5,000 troops waiting for the ships stayed in a nearby transit camp on the outskirts of Harwich.

The camp had been built in 1945-'46 by German POWs. The prisoners were taken down to the ship by truck which brought back returnees. Carefully coordinated train schedules in the UK and in Europe provided an interlocking continuous service. All mail to and from the B.A.O.R. was also carried in these ships. *Empire Parkeston* and the *Vienna* alternated, with *Empire Wansbeck* serving as back-up in case of need and when one or the other was off on annual care and maintenance.

Empire Parkeston continued on this rather monotonous back and forth service for almost 16 years, mostly making night crossings, which made seaman service in her not the most popular of GSNC ships' service as it resulted in very rare nights at home for her crew. Due to all the military passengers and the continuous trips, there was a considerable crew of 87, including 4 deck and 10 engineering officers, two radio officers, two military Masters-At-Arms for policing duties, and a permanent Dutch pilot to take them in and out of Hoek van Holland. She could carry 813 troops on the "bleak and gloomy troop decks" in four and five-tier bunks. As well there were 182 cabins, accommodating two to 11 persons, for female troops, officers, families and traveling civilian officials. No meals were served to troops or passengers, but N.A.A.F.I. (the familiar, to naval types, Navy, Army Air Force Institute) provided a pay as you go major canteen service. There were saloons forward for the men and aft for the officers and families, special rooms for mothers and infants, a fully staffed hospital, and "even the troop decks were air conditioned." To save money, and as the crossing time was more than adequate, she usually operated with only two of her four boilers, sufficient for 16-17 knots.

Empire Parkeston in her troop transport role at the Hook of Holland Courtesy of L.L. von Munching Wassenaar, Holland

Empire Parkeston in her final form with the Transport Service dark blue and Thornycroft funnel tops in the late 1960s Author's collection

It was in reality a strenuous life, at least for the watch officers. The ship sailed from Parkeston Quay each night shortly before midnight, arriving at the Hook by 7 a.m. the next morning (dense fog permitting), sailing again to return at 10 p.m. The Master took her out of Harwich and turned over to the duty Mate off the Sunk light vessel for the 116-mile crossing and retired to sleep on a couch in the chartroom, while Mates shared the night watches. Although the Dutch pilot took the *Parkeston* in and out of the New Waterway to the Hook quays, the Master was always beside him on the bridge. It was a very busy part of the North Sea, with numerous other ships and small fishing vessels to avoid. Also, a Mate notes, they had to watch for the large civilian ferry SS *Amsterdam*, which left the Hook an hour later than the *Parkeston* but was to overtake them by the Sunk light vessel. The *Amsterdam's* schedule required her to arrive at Parkeston Quay to connect with a fast boat train and was not to be delayed. If, as not infrequently happened, *Amsterdam* was late, the *Parkeston*, for some unknown engineering reason, rather than just stopping and waiting, would circle around at modest speed until the other ship appeared and went on into Harwich. Returning troops were apparently less important than

Three Princes Armed

paying passengers and waiting passenger trains! Each year she went down to London, Hull, or another sea port for annual survey and inspection. In February 1952 the *Empire Parkeston*, when coming alongside in the Hook had a steering engine failure and demolished one of the *Wansbeck's* lifeboats and its davits. But delays in service were very rare. At one stage the tops of her funnels were modified to a Thornycroft design to help keep smoke off the bridge, and she was repainted in light grey with a distinguishing HMT narrow blue band along the hull.

But by 1961, with the cut-back in British Forces in Europe and the rising costs of all the trains involved in both countries, and with the *Parkeston's* rather large crew, the whole operation became an economic millstone. Experiments were tried operating the ship from other ports – Cardiff, Plymouth, Southampton, Dover and others - which was popular with the troops at least. At the time of the Suez crisis in 1956-57 the ship was again employed in "real" trooping, going to the Mediterranean with soldiers and making trips between Cyprus and Port Said. She then returned to cross-Channel trooping for another four years.

However, with the ship now over 30 years old, she (and the other three troopers as well) was withdrawn, arriving for the last time at Harwich on 26 September, 1961, dressed overall and flying the traditional long paying-off pennant. Her Master, "Billy" James, had made more than 1,000 trips and retired with the ship, which had made 1,100 crossings between 1947 and 1961. The ship trooping service was largely to be replaced by air service. And the three troopers on this run had carried upwards of eight million passengers – a major contribution. The ship lay in the River Stour at a mooring just off the ferry piers for a few months, soon looking somewhat rust streaked and forlorn, while a purchaser was sought.

The *Parkeston*, ex-*Prince Henry* and *North Star*, was shortly sold to a firm of Italian ship-breakers, Lotti Spa at La Spezia in north-west Italy, 80 km southeast of Genoa. She was towed there by the

Dutch tug *Gele See* arriving on 29 February 1962 and broken up during the year. As far as can be traced, not even her last ship's bell has survived, but the *Henry* had led a highly varied and useful career.

CHAPTER EIGHT

Prince David and Prince Robert Go Back To Civvie Street

I have been young, and now am not too old;
And I have seen the righteous forsaken,
His health, his honour and his quality taken…
　　　　Edmund Blunden "Report on Experience" (1929)

BY JUNE 1945 WITH THE WAR IN EUROPE ended and *Prince Henry* already in British hands, the Canadian Navy informed the Admiralty that they were only prepared to man and send *Prince Robert* for duties in the Pacific, which was done. Thus it was agreed in June that, as Canada didn't require *Prince David*, the Landing Ship could be transferred to the Royal Navy. However she was lying at the naval facilities in Esquimalt, B.C. after being released from dockyard hands, where she had been in part modified for possible employment in the Pacific campaign. Before an Admiralty decision was reached on her use, the Japanese war ended in August, and the vessel was transferred back to Canadian ownership. But she was surplus to Canada's post-war requirements, and thus there needed to be a decision as to her fate. She lay waiting at Esquimalt while various options were considered, including retaining her, or at least one of the *Princes*, in the Navy. This went on until the beginning of January 1946. Then, the Navy having passed on that idea, she was towed around to what some called "the naval bone-yard" at Lynn Creek, North Vancouver on the mainland where lay several other surplus warships.

HMCS *Prince Robert*, which had returned to Esquimalt on 20 October from her foray to Hong Kong, held a couple of publicity "Open Houses", then had her armament and secret naval equipment like coding machines and some radar removed. In early January 1946, manned only by a small maintenance crew, she too was towed by three naval tugs to Lynn Creek and paid off to lie alongside her sister ship *Prince David*. In early January 1946 both were transferred to the Government's War Assets Corporation (WAC) for disposal. WAC published "For Sale By Tender" notices in various shipping journals, offering the two *Princes* for sale "as is, where is," but noting that "Both ships were completely refitted in June, 1945, were found to be in good condition throughout" and that "Maintenance is constantly being carried out and the machinery turned over periodically." Given their state later, this would seem to be stretching the facts to some extent. Their initial suggested asking price was $500,000 each.

The CNR was asked by War Assets if they would like to reacquire their ships. But once bitten twice shy. Given the ships' prewar unprofitability, their age now of 16 years, hard wartime use and the prohibitive cost of converting them back to civilian use it was a hard sell. After considerable back and forth correspondence between the CN, War Assets and the Navy as well, nothing was being decided. By this time there were a multitude of corvettes, frigates, minesweepers and other warships available for disposal to any buyer, so the two *Princes* did not warrant unusual sales effort by War Assets.

Finally Robert C. Vaughan, the CNR's President (and *Robert's* possible namesake according to some) declined as did the Navy and WAC had to look elsewhere for a potential buyer. The CN was still to employ another *Prince* ship on the B.C. coastal trade for many years. That was *Prince George*, somewhat smaller and with a single funnel, but quite similar to their pre-war vessels.

Greek firms were anxious to re-enter the shipping trades. They were short of vessels due to wartime losses where they had suffered mightily. Anticipating considerable post-war demand for transport out of devastated Europe, they were approached or responded to the ads (records don't indicate which), and the two ships were shortly committed for sale to the London-based Charlton Steam Shipping Company, a recently acquired subsidiary of the Greek Chandris Lines. *Prince David* was bought for $375,000 on 7 January and *Prince Robert* for the same amount on 18 January 1946, after some three months of negotiations.

However they remained in Canada until February 1947, and Canadian Jack C. Dosie was engaged as a local advisor for Charlton. He managed to convince Charlton that the two ships were indeed a practical concept for their plans, hired local civilian crews on a temporary basis and the two ships eventually sailed under their own power for Southampton via the Panama later that month. All of the changes, modifications and re-assignments of duties in the past seven years meant that plans and drawings for those operating the machinery often didn't match reality. Her 4th Engineer for the trip across, John Henderson, found that a large pipe passing through the engineroom and into both No.1 boiler room ahead and No.2 boiler room aft was blanked off at both ends – doing nothing, a left-over from some previous change. He writes that this was not uncommon both with piping and electrical circuits. As one engineroom hand said "It was like a bowl of spaghetti!" Continuing to some extent her history of misfortunes, in *Prince David* there was even a minor engineroom fire when she was in Curaçao on the way across.

They both were then sent by Charlton Shipping over to the Belgian yard of Beliard, Crighton & Cie. (subsequently Beliard Murdoch S.A.) at Antwerp for reconversion to civilian passenger use which took more than a year. The plans for conversion after a

Charlton Sovereign ex-Prince Robert at Antwerp for trials 1949 Author's
collection

careful examination were prepared by a British firm, Esplen, Son &
Swainston of London. The yard noted in a letter to the author that
the boiler and enginerooms "were, of course, in a deplorable state
of dirtyness", but that "the turbines were found in rather good condition… but required serious overhaul." They too noted that they
had practically no drawings, and that "those that were available
did not correspond with the reality. Our people spent a couple of
weeks not only tracing pipelines but also in trying to find out what
they were needed for." They too found the blanked off heavy pipe
that led nowhere. It is only fair to note that the initial 1940 conversions and then many modifications and refits were made under the
high pressure of wartime urgency, and if drawings and records were
not up to peacetime standards, it is not hard to understand why.
Conversion costs by Beliard alone were $520,064 (US) for *Prince
David* and $666,021 for *Prince Robert*, most of the difference being
due to changes in safety regulations, sanitary and air conditioning
requirements during the latter's conversion.

Prince David was re-named *Charlton Monarch* and *Prince Robert Charlton Sovereign* during their refit to civilian status. Two-inch armour plate, gun shelters and platforms, and the heavy LCA davits in *David* were removed. They retained their cut-down superstructure and two funnels, but both required considerable strengthening to meet British Ministry of Transport and Lloyd's Insurers regulations, and added safety requirements in both controls and for watertight bulkhead improvements. Both ships were destined specifically for Charlton's emigrant trade under the auspices of the Switzerland-based I.R.O. – International Refugee Organization, sponsored by the United Nations. This organization were offering subsidized fares to those in Europe who now had no homes or wished to escape the devastation, and Charlton obtained a charter contract for the minimum of a year.

By today's standards the accommodation for some 750 passengers planning to travel between Europe and Africa to South America and Australia was pretty basic. All male passengers, and most female as well were put up in large dormitories for 20 to 40 people. The UK magazine "Shipbuilding And Shipping Record" for 5 May 1949 commented blandly that "While austere, as befits these times, maximum room is provided in these dormitories and bunks of latticed steel construction from hygienic and fire danger considerations are extremely comfortable." The facilities for female passengers were separate and somewhat smaller. There were hospitals for both sexes and an operating room and facilities for "infectious cases." All this reduced at least *Charlton Monarch's* gross tonnage by some 350 tons, and she was calculated to steam at a more modest 15 knots (from her designed speed of up to 22 knots) for up to 6,000 miles.

For Charlton Lines, the *Charlton Monarch* could really only be described as a disaster. On her maiden, and only, voyage under her new house flag she sailed on 16 May 1948 from Bremerhaven in north Germany. Four vessels left about the same time, with 758 in *Charlton Monarch*, 4,858 in total. They were to a large extent Mennonites, 667 in the *Monarch*, from a refugee camp at Gronau on the German-Dutch border. These unfortunates had already fled anticipated persecution by advancing Russians. Under I.R.O. auspices most of these people were headed for Paraguay in central South America to set up self-contained towns there. In 1929 they had before this fled Russia into Germany, and were now refugees again.

Charlton Monarch set off across the Atlantic, just like in old wartime days, for South America. She put in to St. Vincent in the West Indies with boiler trouble, then continued south. But off Pernambuco Province, Brazil, near Recife, she had a major boiler problem which this time resulted in an engineroom turbine failure. When rescued the ship was drifting helplessly off that port. Beliards notes defensively in their description of the conversion (in April 1970) that the "failure was being attributed to Engineer's negligence (this as far as we know however.)"

She was discovered at sea by pure chance and towed in to Recife on 9 July by the Falkland Islands-based Antarctic survey ship *John Briscoe* on its way for an annual survey in England. *Charlton Monarch* lay alongside while her problem and unwelcome passengers were sorted out. They were not allowed ashore as none had any landing rights in Brazil. It was only a few degrees south of the equator, and a Chief Officer from another ship who went aboard, having remembered *Prince David* from his youth in B.C., reported she was dreadfully overcrowded, filthy dirty and the air conditioning was unserviceable. No record has been located as to what happened to the passengers, presumably transported in some other vessel that Charlton would have chartered, still aiming for their goal over 1,400 miles farther south to Brazil and then another 600 miles inland to Paraguay. A tale of suffering over decades that has escaped any significant notice.

After trials at repairing the ship, it was found to be impossible in Recife, so *Charlton Monarch* set off under tow by the Dutch tug *Zeelandia*. But even that was disrupted by engine troubles with the tug, which struggled with her tow into Las Palmas in the Canaries. There she was taken over by another Dutch vessel, *Tyne*, and was towed back to the Clyde by 1 October, and then down to Barry Docks in Wales. There the *Monarch* lay to a mooring fore and aft with other desolate vessels for some time, now assessed as not being worth the major costs of repairs. Even here ill fortune dogged the ship for a couple of workmen were asphyxiated during work on her. Abandoned to the insurers by Charlton Shipping, over the course of three years she was gradually dismantled with, as John Gwilliam of Swansea reported, parts being cannibalized to keep the other two, *Empire Parkeston* and *Charlton Sovereign* operating. She seems to have lasted afloat for those years, for she is finally reported as being broken up at the South Wales shipbreakers in Briton Ferry, to the west near Swansea, in October 1951. A sorry end for a valiant ship. The Charlton company showed a loss of £88,366, about $440,000 at the time, for the year 1948 on this ship alone. They were still on the hook the following year for expenses relative to their contract with the I.R.O. for chartering a substitute vessel for the emigrants they had planned on carrying. Their insurers declared the ship a "constructive total loss" as of 10 June, 1948. The Charlton company eventually recovered but £50,000 from those insurers.

Charlton Sovereign, ex-*Prince Robert*, was a much more successful venture by Charlton. Refitted in the same Beliard yard in Antwerp to essentially the same scale of accommodation, she was also employed in the emigrant trade as planned, taking her first lot of emigrants from Bremerhaven on 4 August, 1948, via Rotterdam, for Sydney, Australia. And *Sovereign* too had boiler problems, both ships due no doubt to hard wartime use with less than perfect maintenance. She was delayed in Gibraltar for a month repairing boilers, and in Batavia, Java with engine problems. Her next voyage was from Bremerhaven to Rio de Janeiro, followed by more engine repairs on the Tyne in England which seem to have at last solved the problems. Then there were three voyages: Naples to Rio, then Naples to Halifax and finally in the series to Central America, all on contract for the I.R.O. She lay alongside idle in Naples for six months, then was sailed to Bremerhaven in 1950 where she lay for a year, pending charters and employing a German crew, which didn't arise. In August 1951, now under management of another Chandris company, Cia. Panameña Europea Navigación Ltda. and under the Panamanian "flag of convenience" she made a pilgrim voyage from Oran to Djeddah, probably appreciated by the Muslim pilgrims who were used to much more primitive and temporarily fitted transports than even these emigrant ships.

On October 1951 *Charlton sovereign* sailed to Genoa, having been bought for a reported $1,367,000 by the major Italian shipping line Fratelli Grimaldi Sicula Oceanica S.A., (one of the Grimaldi-Siosa group of companies), who were also much involved in the emigrant trade through the I.R.O. After quite an expensive and extensive refit she became the most modern of their fleet of usu-ally elderly (and cheap) vessels. *Charlton Sovereign* was renamed *Lucania* in their service. At the shipyard her bow was extended some 15 feet, giving a much sharper rake than before. Provision was made for considerable first class accommodation forward as she now could accommodate 170 first class passengers in fully and elegantly fitted cabins, reportedly a first for Grimaldi, as well as the original 800 tourist class. Brochures were produced advertis-ing ports of call at Cannes, Barcelona, Tenerife in the Canaries, La Guaira at Curaçao and Pointe à Pitre. One writer, Peter Eisele of Chatham, New Jersey, says "Internally the *Lucania's* public rooms were gaudy to say the least. Furnishings were ultra-modern and (could) be described as psychedelic today. The first class saloon, for instance, had contour chairs in shades of green and yellow, with wall drapes of red and blue and a ceiling light fixture of every colour imaginable."

Three Princes Armed

Lucania at Naples July 1953 Courtesy Commander Aldo Fraccaroli

Lucania ex-Prince Robert Courtesy Commander Aldo Fraccaroli

For Fratelli Grimaldi she worked well with few reported problems, mostly in their service between Italy, the Caribbean, Central and South America. Sailing from home base in Genoa she made a continuous series of trips to these various ports for nine years. But emigrant services dropped off, Grimaldi found that the future lay in more upper class travel and began to purchase and carefully refit larger veteran liners. Finally, over 30 years old and well worn, *Lucania/Prince Robert* was scrapped at Vado, near Leghorn, in 1962.

If one counts the three ships' pre-war services, even allowing for the financial difficulties of the depression, and their wartime contributions around the globe, followed, in two of the three cases by further valiant and economically satisfactory contributions to world travel, it was a contribution of which Sir Henry Thornton could have been reasonably proud, despite his shabby treatment by the Canadian Government.

As Sir Francis Drake's prayer before attacking Cadiz in April 1587 puts it in part:

> *"O Lord God, when thou givest thy servants to endeavour any*
> *great matter,*
> *grant us also to know that it is not the beginning but the continuing*
> *of the same*
> *until it be thoroughly finished which yieldeth the true glory…"*

Epilogue

But if he be poorer than thy estimation, then he shall present himself
before the priest, and the priest shall value him: according to his
ability, that vowed shall the priest value him.

Leviticus, Ch. 27, v.8

HOW CAN WE ASSESS THE VALUE of these three *Prince* ships? They led three wildly varied lives, with only two, *Prince Henry* and *Prince Robert* living out their anticipated normal span. But *ex post facto* assessments are always clearer.

As CNR's ferries and cruise ships, the times were against them before they sailed from their builder's hands. As Cammell Laird feared, they were somewhat too large and too costly for their roles on the B.C. coast. Rather like using a Cadillac as a taxi under the circumstances. It does its job perfectly, but the investment is not worth it. Their speed advantage over the CP's *Princess* ships, while a selling point for Sir Henry Thornton's presentation to his Board in 1928, was to work against them when operating costs became a more major factor. Shades of gasoline economies now becoming an advantage even for family cars. If the depression had not intruded, there are indications that another three ships, or even two of them, added to the Triangle Run between Vancouver, Victoria and Seattle were more than the traffic required or could be developed unless the CP withdrew. That was a highly unlikely event given the competitive challenges of the day and the two protagonists – CPR's Beatty and the CN's Thornton. And Beatty's ships had remained on the job, and presumably generated passenger awareness even if not loyalty on a continuous basis after the CN withdrew in 1922.

While one can sympathise with Thornton in his strongly held objective of aspiring to compete wherever his opponent operated, these ships were overkill in their sphere. In the end it was the CNSS service that was killed, within the year. The concept of passenger shipping competition between the two was not a bad one except for the timing, given the *Lady* boats successes on the Atlantic. But those east coast vessels had the added advantage of space for considerable commercial cargoes backed by a long standing government agreement for trade connections with the Caribbean islands. The *Princes* now would seem at the least to have been in the wrong place – at the time. But then things were buoyant when Sir Henry made his proposal, and even most economists did not forecast the upcoming disaster. Although unlikely, it might have been.

As cruise ships they were much more satisfactory. But again the slacking demand resulting from the depression meant that three were too many. One ship, to Alaska and then on the Atlantic coast, maybe, but hardly room for three. It was an ambivalent time – demand for cruises only slowly recovering, the ships on the small side for any serious notoriety as cruise liners like *Queen of Bermuda*. In themselves they seem to have been popular and were certainly elegantly comfortable and a pleasure in which to travel.

Fortunately occasional use in various cruising roles and as very minor players meant there was a call for their services. That call was sufficient to, if not make a profit, at least come close and prevent their sale, whatever the Navy recommended. *Prince Robert* came closest to being a satisfactory investment, *Henry* was at best marginal, and her sale to Clarke Steamship Ltd. was fortuitous. *David*, with a tendency to go aground, have engine break-downs, (and later hit a mine) can only be assessed as a CN, sometimes naval and certainly Charlton Shipping millstone. Not necessarily the ship's own fault, but it is hard to separate ship and Master. When one looks at the massive 2,800-passenger cruise "liners" of today (what one critic called "a floating block of flats"), the *Princes* were quite satisfactory in their more intimate role. If demand had further recovered they might have led reasonably useful lives, in someone's hands, if not the CNSS's. Watching the *North Star* in Pictou Harbour, she seemed a bit much for smaller ports like that, but in those late 1930s the organizers needed the attraction of something different to entice new customers. It was what is now called a niche market.

As naval vessels the assessment is a bit more difficult, partly as a result of the ships' varying roles. As Armed Merchant Cruisers they had some advantages, and the one considerable disadvantage from which all AMCs suffered. In reality they could not reasonably have taken on any of the very well armed German raiders, certainly not the large armoured ships, given the examples of the larger and overwhelmed *Jervis Bay, Rawalpindi* and others. In fact the average British AMCs were twice as large as the *Princes* (at an average of 15,100 grt. versus the Princes' nominal 7,000), and even they suffered the same lack of ability against their likely foes. They were of little use against U-boats, except that we often forget that most U-boat attacks were made on the surface. While the *Princes* would likely have succumbed to torpedoing (10 of 16 lost RN AMCs were to U-boat torpedoes), their guns were a viable threat to any surfaced submarine. Their use as troop convoy escorts in the early days in the Pacific and in the Atlantic was reasonable and proper, given that the enemy would probably be a raider who could ill afford any damage so far from home, and, it was hoped, would draw off in the face of an armed escort.

A major asset was that psychologically they lent heart to those convoyed – a competent looking armed warship as a protector. Even the lowly corvettes, in too few numbers for their Atlantic convoys, did the same, providing the almost defenceless merchantmen at least the illusion of armed protection. After all, as the Convoy Instructions said, the primary aim was "The safe and timely arrival of the ships," not sinking enemies. On the West Coast one of the declared aims was to show the local populace that they were protected from the sea and possible attack by the marauding Japanese.

It was indeed fortunate that the latter never tested the theory, but to see a 7,000-ton armed warship come into port no doubt gave considerable comfort, and took some pressure off the naval administration to provide more seaward defence when the primary worry was elsewhere. Only the *cognoscenti* may have had their doubts. Better Asdic fits would have helped possibly, but these were not intended as A/S ships in any role.

As Landing Ships Infantry the two, *David* and *Henry* performed their most valuable roles, and in a manner that was entirely adequate for the requirements of the day. The right ships of the right type and size for the jobs and locations, at Normandy and Toulon, in Italy and Greece. Here their previous roles as passenger ferries at last paid off, and crew and soldiers alike had no quibbles with their abilities and performances. In fact they were under-used due to the generous allowance of shipping and the scarcity of losses. But that did not make them less valuable. Later, in Greek waters, *Henry* and *David* did yeoman service to some extent in their original roles as passenger carriers, for Greek and British troops, for escaping civilians, and in returning Italian POWs to their homeland. They often carried far more than their designed capacity, but seemed almost ideal for the service.

Prince Robert as an AA cruiser was fully satisfactory, although a bit on the light side for armament, and slower than her contemporaries such as the RN's elderly AA cruisers. She was really only firmly tested once and coped as expected. More opportunities, somewhat heavier guns, might have further proven her unique, in the RCN, value. At Hong Kong in September '45 she was ideal – well armed, looked belligerent and carried sufficient seamen to land significant parties for dockyard control. Given the background of many of the Prisoners Of War, it was reportedly heart-stoppingly opportune that a major Canadian warship was back to rescue them. A serious error in judgement may have put the prisoners there, but Canada was back to rescue them, with one of the same ships. The other original ship, SS *Awatea*, was sunk in the Mediterranean in November 1942. *Robert's* participation was an exceptional gesture.

MacLeod in his 1965 paper makes several more general points outlining these ships' naval contributions. "They provided for Canada a naval entry into the wider stages, a wider scope for the RCN" (than its acknowledged contribution to convoy A/S warfare and destroyer operations, usually with the RN). "They provided a flexibility, a balance for Canada's fleet in the exercise of sea power," and they provided the more senior officers with sea and operational commands. Like the rest of the RCN, these ships helped to build a naval tradition upon civilian foundations. Canada was not <u>just</u> a "Corvette Navy," with ships commanded by young Lieutenants and Lieutenant Commanders. Maybe untested, the *Princes* were sufficient for their time in roles beyond the main ones Canada accepted. A note in all the responses received is that their crews, officers and men, were proud of them, and felt they were making a real contribution to the freedom of the seas. These three had helped make the RCN a somewhat well rounded fleet, an addition to the small aircraft carriers we manned, *Nabob* and *Puncher*, and the two cruisers, *Uganda* and *Ontario*, operated in the last few months of the war.

Post war, when the three got going again in the hands of others, *Prince Henry* as *Empire Parkeston* contributed 17 years sterling service to the British Transport Services. With no more than normal problems, she served unspectacularly year after year. As the naval officers' personal assessment form S-206 used to say "To my entire satisfaction." She lasted in her four roles for 32 years, longer than many ships in easier jobs, so with her as the measure, Cammell Laird could be well satisfied with what they had produced.

Prince David as *Charlton Monarch* is best forgotten. Maybe her engines should have been replaced after her histories of serious groundings, floodings and being mined, an aftersight that was probably not economically feasible. *Prince Robert* – *Charlton Sovereign*

- *Lucania* served out her time for almost 32 years as well, and evidently to Fratelli Grimaldi's satisfaction as well.

For *Henry* and *Robert* their relatively long latter roles were probably proof of their place in maritime history. Right sized ships in the right roles in the right trades for the day. If one adds the two brief times in the sun for the Landing Ships Infantry, it is not a bad return, even if their originators, the CNR, soon saw them as nothing but millstones. But then the depression was no-one's fault.

This history has recorded the contributions of three *Princes*, many of them, to Canada's maritime role over the years from 1930 to 1962. Not enough is known of that role. This fills in some blank spaces on the canvas.

> *"See that ye hold fast the heritage we leave you, yea and teach your children its value, that never in the coming centuries their hearts may fail them or their hands grow weak"*
> *Attributed to Sir Francis Drake*

Credits

Chapters 1 & 2:

Maurice Beaudet, Mgr. – Shipping Fleet, Clarke Steamship Co. Ltd., Montreal, correspondence with FM McKee, 1968

CN Archives, via web site, 2007

Canadian National Railways Magazine, March, 1930 to August 1932, CNR

Wayne Cook to the F M McKee, 1970

E.H. Dodd, Cammel Laird & Co., Birkenhead, correspondence & Company magazine (May, 1963), to FM McKee, 1967

The Empire Club of Toronto, 1922 Addresses, Sir Henry Thornton, 11 Dec. 1922

Kevin Griffin, e-mail correspondence with FM McKee, 2005

John Henderson, Victoria, correspondence with FM McKee, 2001

Dr. Ken S. Mackenzie, CNR historian, Ottawa (1992, correspondence)

D'Arcy Marsh "The Tragedy of Henry Thornton", MacMillan Co., Toronto, 1935

National Archives Canada, RG12, v.1096, File 11-32-10 re initial costs and DAVID's stranding, 1932.

Journal of the Puget Sound Maritime History Society, Seattle, (1930, 1945, 1967)

Lloyd M. Stadum, Research Chairman Puget Sound MARIST Society (1970 correspondence)

James T. Rice, Seattle, correspondence with FM McKee, 1968

A.C. Simpson, North Vancouver, correspondence with FM McKee, 1970

Brian Singleton, Editor, "Shipbuilding & Shipping Record", London (1970)

University of Pennsylvania Archives, Nancy R. Miller; Philadelphia, to F M McKee, Feb.2007

Victoria "Times-Colonist – The Islander", January-February, 1982 (Don Stevens)

Chapters 3, 4, 5 & 6

Jack W. Aldred, letter to F.M. McKee, 2000

C.P.O. Douglas Allen, Interview with RA Darlington, 1999

LCdr Norm Anderson, discussions with RA Darlington, Victoria, 2007

Richard Bentham, e-mail to FM McKee 16 April 1999

Carl Boyd & Akihiko Yoshida "The Japanese Submarine Force And World War II," US Naval Institute, Annapolis, MD, 1995

Dacre Cole, Interview with RA Darlington 1999

Conway's All The Worlds Fighting Ships, 1980

Rear Admiral W.B. Creery, correspondence with FM McKee 1970

The Crowsnest, the RCN magazine "Prize Money," date nk

The Crowsnest, the RCN magazine "Prince Henry's Half Victory," date nk

LCdr Jack Davie DSC, correspondence with FM McKee, 1993-94

Rear Admiral C.J. Dillon, Interview with RA Darlington, Victoria, 1998

Alec Douglas, Roger Sarty, Michael Whitby et al, "A Blue Water Navy", and "No Higher Purpose," Vanwell Publishing, St Catharines, 2007 & 2002

Robert M. Dundas, letter to FM McKee 6 August, 1999

Stoker Howard Eames, letter to FM McKee, 1999

Commander Kenneth Edwards, "Operation Neptune" 1946

Jim Francis, letter to RA Darlington, 5 August 1999

David Freeman, "Canadian Warship Names", Vanwell Publishing, St Catherines, 2000

The Globe and Mail, Toronto - Kenneth Cambon obituary, 17 March 2007

Captain Val S. Godfrey, letter to FM McKee, 17 June 1967

Commodore John W.F. Goodchild, correspondence with FM McKee, 1997

Mr. Justice Donald E. Graham, interview with FM McKee, Toronto, 2007

Captain Vern W. Howland, letter to FM McKee, March 1968

George Herring, letter to FM McKee, 13 November 1999

Rear Admiral F.L. Houghton, "Memoir", 1980

Commander Ron Jackson, letter to FM McKee, 1968

Lieutenant Bill Johnson, "The Prince Robert", VIP Graphic Studio, Sidney, B.C., 1988

Lieutenant Bill Johnson, Interview with RA Darlington, Victoria 1999

Dr. James O. Kaufman, Memoirs, November 1999

Captain T.D. Kelly, conversations with FM McKee, 1969

Paul Kemp, "U Boats Destroyed" US Naval Institute, 1997

H.T. Lenton, "German Surface Vessels Vol. 2", Doubleday, London, 1966

David Lewis, Len Birkenes & Kit Lewis, "Naval Combined Operations," (privately published memoirs) 1998

Billy Lindsay, interview with RA Darlington 1999

Cdr. George MacFarlane, interview with RA Darlington Victoria 1999

John M. MacFarlane, "Canada's Admirals and Commodores," Maritime Museum of BC 1994

Lieutenant (E) John L. Maw, interview with RA Darlington, Victoria, 1999

Harold Moist, interview with RA Darlington, Victoria, 1996

The Naval & Military Museum of Alberta

The Naval & Military Museum of Esquimalt

Edward O'Connor, letter to FM McKee, 2001

Osborne, Richard 'Armed Merchant Cruisers 1878 –1945"

NOAC, The Ottawa Branch, "Salty Dips Volume 3" 1988

NOAC, The Ottawa Branch, "Salty Dips Volume 6" 1999

NOAC, The Ottawa Branch, "Salty Dips Volume 8" 2001

Cdr. E.R. Paquette & Lt. C.G. Bainbridge, "Honours and Awards - Canada's Naval Service - WWII," E.W. Bickle Ltd., Victoria, 1986

Rear Admiral H.A. Porter, letter to FM McKee 10 October 1999

Jurgen Rohwer, "Axis Submarine Successes 1939-1945," US Naval Institute, 1983

Theodore Roscoe, "US Destroyer Operations WWII," US Naval Institute, 1953

Captain S.W. Roskill, "The War At Sea, Vol. I," Her Majesty's Stationery Office, London, 1954

Captain S.W. Roskill, "The War At Sea, Volume III Part 1" Her Majesty's Stationery Office, London 1960

Joseph Schull, "The Far Distant Ships," King's Printer, Ottawa, 1952

Captain W. Geoff Shedden, correspondence & interviews with FM McKee, 1968

Leading Seaman Ernest Smedley, letters and photographs to FM McKee June, 1999

Larry Stebbe, Interview with RA Darlington, Victoria, 2007

John Stroud, telephone interview with FM McKee, Toronto, 2007

Time Magazine, 4 December 1950

Able Seaman Neil Tomlinson, letters to FM McKee January and September, 1984

Gilbert Tucker, "The Naval Service of Canada Vol. II," King's Printer, Ottawa, 1952

The Victoria Daily Colonist, 25 September 1977

Leading Seaman William Welsh, Letter to FM McKee 15 May 1999

Commander Alf Wurtele, correspondence with FM McKee 1968

Chapters 7 & 8:

Alewijnse, Northville, MI., article in "Great Eastern Journal" (UK), GER, 2005

Douglas Brown, Harwich, Essex, correspondence in 2007 re EMPIRE PARKESTON

Anthony Cooke, "Emigrant Ships", Carmania Press, London, (n.d. – c.1993)

Peter Eisele, Chatham, N.J. letter to FM McKee, 8 Feb. 1970

Global Anabaptist Mennonite Encyclopedia web site, 2007

Ken Griffin, e-mails to FM McKee

John Gwilliam, Swansea, Wales, letter to FM McKee, Jan. 1970

G.L. Harvey, "On the Harwich-Hook Trooping Run", in "Sea Breezes" Magazine, (n.d., Dec.,1980's)

John Henderson, Victoria, letters to FM McKee, Jan. 2001.

Robert I. Hendy, Toronto (late CMDRE, RCNR), Toronto, conversations with FM McKee

Captain W.G. James, GSNC, London, unpublished memoir, Oct. 1969

William H. Miller, "Chandris Liners", Carmania Press, London, 1993

Adrian Monk, San Carlos, Falklands, letter to FM McKee, 1970

William Paulus, Massillon, Ohio, letter to FM McKee, 10 Feb. 1970

"Shipbuilding & Shipping Record", UK for 5 May 1949

Giorgio Spazzapan, Ferrania, Italy, letter to FM McKee, 4 Feb. 1970

P. Sunderland, Keighley, Yorkshire, letter to FM McKee, 27 Jan.1970

"Vancouver Sun" for 8 May, 1962

H. van der Lugt, Netherlands, letter to FM McKee, 9 Jan.1970

L.L. von Münching, Wassenaar, Netherlands, letter to FM McKee, 3 Apr. 1970

G. Vercruyssen, Manager, Beliard Murdoch S.A., Antwerp, letter to FM McKee 3 April 1970

S.A. Wass, letter, "Sea Breezes" Magazine, (n.d.,1980s)

Biographical Note:

Captain (N) Robert A. Darlington was born in Winnipeg. In 1948 he joined the Canadian Navy as a Sub Lieutenant in the Supply Branch. He served in the Regular Force at sea in HMCS *Beacon Hill* and HMCS *Gatineau*, in supply, training and secretariat positions in Canada, Italy, the US, and with NATO, retiring in 1982. He returned to Winnipeg as the DND Regional Audit Director, retiring from that in 1987 and moved to Victoria. In 1996 he first collaborated with Commander McKee in writing "The Canadian Naval Chronicle", published by Vanwell Publishing in St. Catherines, which went to a 2nd edition in 1998. It was a carefully and fully researched volume on every one of the RCN's successes and losses in WW II, and is widely used as a reliable reference.

Commander Fraser M. McKee joined the RCNVR in Toronto in 1943, and remained in the Reserves until 1975, specializing in anti-submarine warfare. He served in the Atlantic in Armed Yachts, and an Algerine escort, returning to Toronto in 1946. He took a degree in forestry, then was employed in the communications industry until retirement in 1984. He became editor of two naval newsletters, then began writing Canadian naval history. He has published five books other than the "Canadian Naval Chronicle": on naval Reserves in Canada, on mine warfare, on one ship - "HMCS Swansea – The Life and Times of a Frigate", on the Armed Yachts, and a companion volume to the "Chronicle" on the loss of the 67 Canadian registered merchant ships and fishing vessels in the Second War, which has received two Honourable Mentions for maritime history. He has written numerous naval articles and contributes book reviews to various publications. He is a past president of the Navy League of Canada, and lives in Toronto.

Wartime Commanding Officers Of The Prince Ships

Prince David
Commander W.B. Armit RCNR
    28 December 1940 – 24 March 1941
Commander K.F. Adams RCN
    25 March 1941 – 1 December 1941
Captain V.S. Godfrey RCN
    2 December 1941 – 18 March 1942
A/Lt. Commander T.D. Kelly RCNR
    19 March 1942 – 16 April 1942
Captain V.S. Godfrey RCN
    17 April 1942 – 17 April 1943
Commander T.D. Kelly RCNR
    18 April 1943 – 1 May 1943
Commander T.D. Kelly RCNR
    23 May 1943 – 11 June 1945

Prince Henry
Captain R.I. Agnew RCN
    4 December 1940 – 19 December 1941
Captain J.C.I. Edwards RCN
    20 December 1941 – 31 December 1942
Captain F.L. Houghton RCN
    1 January 1943 – 18 March 1943
Lt. Commander E.W. Finch-Noyes RCN
    19 March 1943 – 22 March 1943
Lt. Commander T.K. Young RCNR
    23 March 1943 – 23 May 1943
Commander T.D. Kelly RCNR
    24 May 1943 – 29 November 1943
Commander K.F. Adams RCN
    30 November 1943 - 11 December 1943
Captain V.S. Godfrey RCN
    12 December 1943 – 13 April 1945

Prince Robert
Commander C.T. Beard RCN
        31 July 1940 – 7 October 1940
Commander F.G. Hart RCN
        8 October 1940 – 21 June 1942
A/Captain F.L. Houghton RCN
        22 June 1942 – 31 December 1942
Commander O.C.S. Robertson RCN
        1 January 1943 – 23 March 1943
Lt. Commander E.W. Finch-Noyes RCN
        24 March 1943 – 5 June 1943
Captain A.M. Hope RCN
        6 June 1943 – 7 December 1944
Captain W.B. Creery RCN
        8 December 1944 – 19 December 1944
Captain W.B. Creery RCN
        4 June 1945 – 10 December 1945

(As listed in "The Ships of Canada's Naval Forces 1910-1993" Ken Macpherson and John Burgess published by Vanwell Publishing Limited, St. Catherines 1994)

INDEX

McRae, D.M. RCAF, 95

Miles Doc Petty Officer, 42

Moist, Harold Petty Officer, 40

Monowai, HMNZS armed merchant cruiser, 51

Monoway, Landing Ship, 132

Monserrate, German blockade runner, 61

Montgomery, Bernard General, 142

MTB 236, 51

Muenchen, German blockade runner, 61

Muni, paul actor, 79

Nagumo, Chuichi Admiral, 78

Nedden, Captain Henry, 19

Nelles, Percy, Vice Admiral, 29

Nene, HMCS frigate, 95

Newcastle, HMS cruiser, 73

Olson, Mr., 103

Ontario, HMCS cruiser, 99

Ontariolite, tanker, 118

Orion, German raider, 47

Osorno, German blockade runner, 49

Papandreou, Georgios Greek Prime Minister, 153

Park, John Lieutenant Winnipeg Grenadiers, 111

Partridge, USS minesweeper, 67

Port Townsend, 25

Portland, German blockade runer, 50

Power, Frank Lieutenant Royal Rifles of Canada, 111

Prahova, German blockade runner, 49

President Garfield, American liner, 51

Princess Beatrix, HMS landing ship, 146

Prins Albert, HMS landing ship, 146

Pritchard, D. Able Seaman, 93

Python, German supply ship, 72

Queen of Bermuda, HMS armed merchant cruiser, 73

Ramsay, Sir Bertram Admiral, 128

Rawalpindi, HMS armed merchant cruiser, 36

Rayburn, Walker correspondent, 169

Reid, Pasquale governor of Easter Island, 53

Robertson, O.C.S. Lieutenant Commander, 38

Ross, John, 5

Ruttan, Mac Lieutenant, 125

Saratoga, USS aircraft carrier, 59

Sartoria, merchant ship, 82

Scharnhorst, German battleship, 35

Schwager, P.G. Surgeon Lieutenant, 138

Seadler, German armed sailing ship, 33

Shedden, W.G. Commander, 70

Sheharazade, French merchant ship, 72

Smith, A.H., 7

Smith, R.K., 30

Snowberry, HMCS corvette, 95

Somers, USS destroyer, 146

St. Margaret, British merchant ship, 72

Stalin, Soviet icebreaker, 54

Stebbe, Larry Lance Corporal Winnipeg Grenadiers, 113

Stroud, John Royal Rifles of Quebec, 113

Surrey, British steamer, 66